The Cuomo Factor

*Assessing the Political Appeal
of New York's Governor*

The Cuomo Factor

*Assessing the Political Appeal
of New York's Governor*

Lee M. Miringoff

Barbara L. Carvalho

Marist Institute for Public Opinion

Marist College

Poughkeepsie, New York

For information:

> Marist Institute for Public Opinion
> Marist College
> Poughkeepsie, New York 12601

Printed in the United States of America

Library of Congress Cataloging in Publication Data

Miringoff, Lee M., 1951-
    The Cuomo Factor.

1. Party affiliation—New York (State) 2. Voting—New York (State) 3. Public opinion—New York (State) 4. Suburbs—New York (State) 5. New York (State)— Politics and government—1951—   . 6. Cuomo, Mario Matthew. I. Carvalho, Barbara L., 1958—   . II. Title. JK2295.N73M57 1986   324.9747   86-62229

ISBN 0-939319-00-4 (pbk)

To
Nancy and Hilda

"It is very difficult making predictions,
especially about the future."

Casey Stengel

About the Authors

Lee M. Miringoff is the Director of the Marist Institute for Public Opinion and is a member of the political science faculty at Marist College, Poughkeepsie, New York. He received his doctorate in political science from M.I.T.

Barbara L. Carvalho is the Director of Research and Data Analysis at the Marist Institute for Public Opinion. She is pursuing her doctoral studies in political science at Fordham University.

TABLE OF CONTENTS

Preface

This study has developed from statewide surveys conducted by the Marist Institute for Public Opinion (MIPO) on Governor Mario Cuomo's performance in office, on New York State politics, and on the political attitudes of the New York electorate. These surveys have revealed Cuomo's extensive popularity among New Yorkers and have identified the basis of his growing political appeal. Mario Cuomo's emergence as a political leader is seen as significant because of the themes he emphasizes, the convincing manner in which he makes his case, and the unusual composition of voters who are responding positively to him.

Since his election as governor of New York in 1982, Mario Cuomo has broadened his base of support beyond the traditional Democratic stronghold of New York City to include the new, pivotal part of the New York State electorate—the New York suburbs. These suburban communities which surround New York City, Nassau and Suffolk counties on Long Island and Westchester and Rockland counties to the north, have undergone tremendous growth and development over recent decades. As a result, the New York State electorate can no longer be considered politically divided into rural-conservative-Republican upstate and urban-liberal-Democratic New York City. But who are these suburban voters and what are their political attitudes?

THE CUOMO FACTOR

What is the relationship that Mario Cuomo has with them?

Conventional wisdom suggests that suburban voters are steadfast Republicans, ideological conservatives, and oppose, for the most part, extensive government intervention into domestic policy. Electoral support for Republican candidates, capped by decisive margins of victory for President Ronald Reagan and Republican Senator Alfonse D'Amato, seems to substantiate this view. Initially, these election results give credence to the thesis advanced in the 1950s that the expansion of suburbia would reinforce its conservative character, provide a safe haven for Republican candidates, and serve as the basis for an eventual party realignment to the GOP. But Democrat Mario Cuomo has achieved significant popularity in the New York suburbs. He has gained the approval of these voters by stressing a positive role for government in domestic policy. Cuomo would appear to be a political anomaly.

In assessing the suburban electorate and Governor Cuomo, this study demonstrates that Mario Cuomo's popularity in the region is not anomalous, but results both from the developments in the suburban communities and from the effectiveness of his approach. This perspective suggests that due to gradual changes in the population and economy of the region, today's suburban electorate is more heterogeneous, more politically independent, and less conservative on government's role in domestic policy than is generally thought. Governor Cuomo, for his part, recognizes the growing role of the region in New York State politics, understands the views of this electorate, and raises issues of concern to these voters.

A relationship has developed between these suburban voters and Mario Cuomo. Suburban voters are familiar with Mario Cuomo's perspective on government and share his viewpoint. Cuomo is perceived as a political figure who advocates government involvement in many social program areas while supporting a pragmatic approach to public policy. This closely matches the suburban voters' preferences. The relationship between the contemporary suburban electorate and Mario Cuomo represents the core of this analysis.

Chapter One discusses Mario Cuomo's growing political appeal. It examines his ability to define the political agenda and to present his positions effectively to the electorate. Emphasis is placed upon the themes he has stressed beginning in 1982, with special attention devoted to his first campaign for governor. In the Democratic primary against New York City Mayor Ed Koch and later, in the general election against Republican Lewis Lehrman, Cuomo demonstrated his abilities. He linked national policy to state politics and established his approach to government's role in addressing domestic policy issues. His subsequent emergence as a political leader has been guided by these themes.

Cuomo's re-election in 1986 was a confirmation of his popularity rather than an introduction of major new approaches. Cuomo's defeat of Republican Andrew O'Rourke by 65% to 32% represented the largest victory for a gubernatorial candidate in New York State's history. Despite the heavy suburban tilt of the GOP slate for the five statewide offices, Cuomo carried all of the four suburban counties surrounding New York City, including Westchester County, the home county of his Republican opponent. His suburban vote was the largest share that a Democratic candidate for governor has received in the region in modern political history.

Chapter Two examines the evolution of New York's suburbs and the unanticipated ways in which they have developed. The pattern of population growth and economic change has created the context for the emergence of a new suburban political landscape. What had been a relatively small, homogeneous region, providing the GOP with large majorities, has developed into a heterogeneous, economically self-contained, and urbanized area with a new political character. The growth of the suburban electorate has enabled it to become a vital partner in New York State politics with the electorates in New York City and upstate.

Chapter Three discusses the present political nature of the New York suburbs, including the political attachments of the electorate and its attitudes on major policy issues. The region has undergone a dramatic rise in Independent identification and a weakening of party ties among partisan identifiers. This decline in partisanship has resulted in greater elasticity in voters' attachments to the political process and in increased selectivity in voters' assessments of politics. Present-day suburban voters are also characterized by their interest in following politics and their concern for issues and candidates.

These trends have resulted in an increase in electoral competition and have provided the opportunity for an effective political appeal by someone like Mario Cuomo. But Cuomo's success here can only be understood following closer examination of this electorate: how does it view itself ideologically and what is its outlook on contemporary issues of public policy. This chapter reveals the changed complexion of suburbia as voters have broadened their issue focus and have proven to be far less conservative than anticipated on issues of government's role in domestic policy.

Chapter Four examines Mario Cuomo's suburban political appeal and this electorate's perception of him. For the most part, these voters see Cuomo as a political leader who represents their viewpoint. They perceive him as progressive and pragmatic: as someone who believes in government involvement in a variety of domestic policy areas, and who, at the same time, is sensitive to budgetary issues. Mario Cuomo's blend of progressive values and pragmatic approaches has gained him the confidence of these voters. As a result, Cuomo presently enjoys the support of many segments of the suburban electorate, extending his political appeal to Independent and moderate voters, while solidifying his popularity with Democrats and liberals. This chapter describes the two-way relationship which has developed in the region. Not only is the suburban electorate familiar with Mario Cuomo's approach and compatible with his views, but Governor Cuomo also understands the political importance of the region and is in touch with contemporary suburban political attitudes.

Chapter Five focuses on political change and the implications of Mario Cuomo's suburban appeal. This chapter suggests that the relationship which has emerged between the suburban electorate and Mario Cuomo is best understood by examining the gradual changes which have occurred in this region and what Mario Cuomo represents to these voters. This analysis of Mario Cuomo's expanding political support in the New York suburbs contrasts with the preponderance of academic and journalistic assessments of national voting trends which have suggested that a party realignment in the direction of the GOP has been occurring. Based upon Republican landslides, narrowing party identification gaps, and conservative movement in the electorate, conclusions about the splintering of the Democratic coalition have often been advanced.

Despite numerous GOP successes, particularly at the presidential level, some narrowing of the gap in Democratic and Republican party identification, and greater dominance of the political agenda by conservative views, this chapter finds that these three factors do not provide a sufficient explanation of current politics. Election outcomes are not a clear measure of realignment; changes in party identification have been misleading, particularly in a relatively partyless era; and, a constituency for continued government involvement in domestic policy remains intact. Although changes have occurred in the electorate, analysis of contemporary American politics should also consider the failure of many Democratic candidates to articulate an approach to public policy which defines the political agenda in terms of government's continued place in society. Their reluctance to do so has cost them dearly at the polls. It is in this context that Mario Cuomo has assumed a leadership role with a political appeal based upon themes which are important to today's electorate.

The data for this study have been drawn from several sources. These include numerous MIPO New York statewide surveys starting with the 1982 campaign for governor and continuing throughout Cuomo's term in office; a major attitudinal survey conducted in the fall of 1985 on the suburban electorate which serves as the data base for Chapters Three and Four; and interviews with Governor Cuomo, several of his aides, and political journalists.

This study is motivated by a desire to examine what are important political developments in the New York suburbs and how Mario Cuomo has attracted wide ranging popularity in the region. In an attempt to gauge voter attitudes, the discussion incorporates survey data in both campaign and non-campaign settings. Assessing the relationship between a political leader and the electorate strictly in a campaign setting can be overly influenced by short-term events and idiosyncracies of the candidates. Reliance upon survey data gathered over time provides an enhanced measure of the basis of that relationship.

Several individuals at Marist College have been particularly helpful. President Dennis J. Murray has been instrumental in the establishment of MIPO and has taken a major interest in MIPO projects. John L. Lahey, Executive Vice President of Marist College, has also played a significant role in the development of MIPO. Anthony J. Cernera, Vice President for College Advancement, has provided guidance in countless ways to both of us, and he has been a source of valuable direction throughout MIPO's growth and in the development of this study. Ann K. Kuhar was the MIPO secretary from 1981-1986. Her contribution to this publication was matched by her assistance in all of MIPO's surveys during that period. Gail Chamberlin, MIPO's current secretary, worked efficiently on later drafts, and Susan Berger, Marist College '86, carried out several research projects associated with this publication. Our appreciation is also extended to: those who agreed to be interviewed for this study; David Hepp and the *Inside Albany* group for their assistance in providing tapes of their programs; and the New York State Board of Elections. A special thanks is extended to Julie Koblenz for her guidance in the technical aspects of publishing, and to Ruth R. Cernera and Matthew S. Greenberg for their editorial assistance.

The talents of hundreds of Marist College students are also reflected in this book. Their dedication has contributed in many ways to this and other MIPO projects. In addition to assisting in the collection of data for these surveys, their participation in numerous classroom discussions is incorporated in this analysis.

Marist Institute for Public Opinion research activities are supported by Marist College, although the analysis contained in this study is that of the authors and does not reflect the opinions of the Institute or the College.

The Cuomo Factor

Assessing the Political Appeal of New York's Governor

Chapter One

The Emergence of Mario Cuomo's Political Appeal

One month before his upset victory in the 1982 Democratic gubernatorial primary over New York City Mayor Ed Koch, then Lieutenant Governor Mario Cuomo was still relatively unknown. An upstate dairy farmer when asked by *The New York Times* about Mario Cuomo replied, "I think she's a strong lady."[1] Cuomo had already held statewide office for eight years.

Campaign strategies for the Democratic nomination were developed in response to the electorate's lack of familiarity with Cuomo. David Hepp of public television's *Inside Albany* noted, "Both Koch's and Cuomo's TV commercials have picked up on what their polls must be telling them about this Cuomo problem. Koch charges 'You don't know him because Cuomo has no record.' Cuomo claims he does and 'The better you know him the more you know he's better for governor.' "[2] Cuomo had a core of support, but he lacked general name recognition. His campaign strategy addressed this basic weakness. Cuomo was a political unknown but not a political novice.

Two years later, Mario Cuomo stood before a prime time television audience at the Democratic National Convention in San Francisco as a highly acclaimed governor. His rousing oratory as the convention's keynote speaker won him rave reviews. *The Washington Post* columnist David Broder noted,

"On keynote night...Cuomo delivered the kind of speech he alone among present-day Democrats seems capable of making. Instantly, the hall filled with talk that 'we're running the wrong man'...Somehow, a supply of 'Cuomo in '88' buttons appeared and became instant best-sellers."[3]

Since the keynote address, speculation about Mario Cuomo's future and possible presidential bid has occupied media attention in Albany and throughout the nation. Network television appearances by Cuomo and national magazine cover stories about him have not been uncommon. Cuomo's re-election to a second term as New York's governor by a record-setting margin that surpassed Grover Cleveland's 1882 winning share has fueled this speculation. But what accounts for Mario Cuomo's growing popularity as governor and his appearance at center stage in the national political spotlight? What distinguishes Mario Cuomo as a political leader in his party and in national politics?

Mario Cuomo's place in contemporary politics cannot be attributed to his electoral track record. Cuomo did not hold elective office until he was nearly fifty and did not succeed in winning an election on his own until 1982. Defeated twice in contests for New York City mayor, his only success, until his gubernatorial primary victory over Ed Koch in 1982 and his narrow defeat of Lew Lehrman in the general election six weeks later, was as part of someone else's ticket. By 1986, when Cuomo won a landslide re-election, he was already a major political figure.

In terms of Cuomo's legislative record, his accomplishments have been noteworthy and have contributed to his political development. As governor, Cuomo mounted a successful campaign for the passage of a transportation bond issue to rebuild New York State's roads and bridges. Other items on his legislative resumé include the passage of a mandatory seatbelt law, legislation raising the alcohol purchase age from 19 to 21, and the enactment of a statewide income tax cut. Despite these accomplishments, Cuomo's legislative record has received criticism. In a news analysis, Michael Oreskes, former Albany bureau chief of *The New York Times,* suggested that Cuomo's reputation is based more on words than deeds. Critics have noted that Cuomo has unusual talents, but "he has not been particularly successful in winning specific legislation or in executing specific programs."[4]

Cuomo claims that enacting legislation takes time. Regarding the legislative process, Cuomo commented, "This is a process I think that you do by accretion, pick up a little piece here, a little piece there, and you have to keep working at it...It took five years to get a medicaid pickup. It took nine years to get them to vote on life imprisonment without parole...It took me two years to get the 21 year old purchase age. Look at all the time it took to get this tax cut, the best tax cut in the history of the state. It took me a long time. So, you don't get everything the first shot."[5] In 1986, Cuomo enjoyed his most productive legislative session by signing bills: opening the way for a state takeover of the Long Island Lighting Company, making it easier for victims of toxic substances to sue the manufacturers, creating a series of economic opportunity zones, settling a medical malpractice insurance dispute, addressing the state liability insurance problem, and placing an environmental bond issue on the 1986 ballot.

But it is neither Cuomo's electoral career nor his legislative accomplishments that set him apart as a political leader. In assessing Mario Cuomo's extensive popularity in New York State and his emergence as a major figure in national politics, this analysis focuses on the Cuomo Factor: namely, Mario Cuomo's ability to understand and define the substance of a political issue, to develop positions which are consistent with his outlook, and to communicate his views effectively. In this regard, the record suggests that Cuomo excels. Through the positions he takes and his ability to articulate his stands, Mario Cuomo has fashioned a balanced approach to government which matches the concerns of today's voters. He has outlined his conception of a positive role for government which involves a new blend of progressive values about government's place in society and pragmatic approaches to public policy. As a result, Mario Cuomo has broadened his support among many groups in New York State, especially among suburbanites who now comprise the swing vote in state politics.

Analyses of Governor Cuomo often concentrate, however, only on his communication skills and not on the themes he emphasizes. These accounts identify Cuomo as "one of the most articulate politicians around"[6] and as Albany's "Great Communicator, the ethnic Ronald Reagan."[7] It has been further noted, "on the rhetoric side, Cuomo remains the king of the hill not only in Albany, probably, but in much of the nation for the Democrats."[8] But Mario Cuomo's skillfulness as a communicator should not be separated from the substance of what he is saying. It is misleading to divorce Cuomo's technique from his message because Mario Cuomo's rise as a political leader is the result of both how he communicates his views and what he addresses. Vice President for NBC News and former Cuomo adviser Tim Russert commented, "It's the positions he takes, and his ability to define the vocabulary that's very important. When you allow the vocabulary to be that social programs are liberal and expensive, it is a loser politically. When you say that the social programs are an extension of the family, that what you bring to your politics and the way you approach government is the same way you run a family, they approve."[9]

There are numerous examples of the Cuomo Factor as it developed beginning with Cuomo's first campaign for governor. One aspect was evident against Ed Koch and Lew Lehrman when

Cuomo demonstrated the ability to define the political agenda and communicate his positions to the voters by linking national policy to state politics. During the height of the recession in 1982 when President Reagan's economic program was unpopular, Cuomo successfully tied Koch, and then Lehrman, to Reaganomics. In so doing, Cuomo placed progressive concerns at the forefront of voters' considerations.

In the 1982 Democratic primary against Ed Koch, Cuomo hammered away at the Reagan economic alternatives, "I think that my candidacy is built on traditional Democratic principles...I am convinced that they work better than the alternatives represented by 'trickle down' and 'supply-side'...I think that this state's tradition...that gave us unemployment insurance and a whole array of strong sound programs was a good one...On the other hand, my opponent believes that government has done too much...He has a new philosophy now, and it is compatible with Ronald Reagan's."[10] In analyzing the first Cuomo-Koch debate, Sidney Schanberg wrote that Cuomo portrayed Koch "as an evolving conservative who had sensed the conservative winds abroad in the land and trimmed his sails accordingly—even toying with his own versions of trickle down economics."[11] In the final primary debate, Cuomo pushed his themes by accusing Koch of " 'embracing' President Reagan's economic philosophy and of displaying 'no difference' between himself and Mr. Lehrman."[12]

In the contest against Lehrman, Cuomo used a similar approach. The ties between Lehrman and Reagan were even more explicit than they were between Koch and Reagan. As Michael Kramer noted, "If Lehrman's tax proposals sound like Reaganomics, it's because Lehrman is a leading guru of the supply-side movement. He long ago broke with the President for straying from the true line, but only a fool would ignore the link to Ronald Reagan's economic policies."[13] Cuomo cornered Lehrman into defending Reagan's economic policy and the supply-side movement. Calling Lehrman the father of Reaganomics, Cuomo charged, "My opponent...not only likes Reaganomics, he wants to go farther."[14]

Cuomo's television commercials stressed these points. They focused on the high unemployment within the state and Lehrman's ties to Reagan. Cuomo's media consultant Harvey Cohen stated, "The jobs commercial [began] by talking about Lew Lehrman saying he wants to create jobs. It then says that the fact is that Lehrman feels Reaganomics doesn't go far enough, and Reaganomics has created the highest unemployment since the Great Depression."[15] A Democratic analyst noted Lehrman's weakness on this point, "no matter how much leeway people are generally willing to give Reagan, the people in New York are fed up with Reaganomics."[16]

The Lehrman campaign was sensitive to this vulnerability as evidenced by the decision not to have President Reagan campaign in the state for Lehrman. Jane Perlez, a reporter for *The New York Times,* wrote that a "Lehrman aide suggested that an appearance by the President could serve to reinforce the campaign theme of Democratic candidate Mario Cuomo."[17] According to Richard Wirthlin, the Reagan and Lehrman pollster, "There are no plans whatsoever to send him [Reagan] to New York now. And I would be very surprised if he visited between now and the election."[18]

Cuomo's strategy of attacking Reagan's supply-side economics was politically well constructed and Cuomo made his case fervently. A pre-election analysis by Frank Lynn of *The New York Times* summarized the issue, "By a 2:1 margin, those surveyed...attributed unemployment in the state to President Reagan rather than any state official. And a majority of those surveyed identified Mr. Lehrman with his fellow Republican, the President, something Mr. Cuomo had sought to promote.

This linkage of candidates and issues [is] a major factor in Mr. Cuomo's lead...."[19]

The worsening economic picture and growing disillusionment with Reaganomics heightened the intensity of the campaign. As one TV commentator remarked, "When unemployment reaches double-digits, politics ceases to be a spectator sport."[20] If the emergence of unemployment as the central campaign issue was particularly helpful to Cuomo, it had the opposite effect on Lehrman's cause. Lehrman had emerged on the political scene during the summer months by running a series of television commercials spelling out his crime program, a major concern for New Yorkers. But as the campaign progressed and unemployment worsened, the economy replaced crime as the number one issue. A pre-election analyst pointed out, "New Yorkers are considerably more concerned about unemployment than about crime, and this is pushing voters more toward Lieutenant Governor Mario Cuomo...Crime is a potent issue for Mr. Lehrman, but not the dominant issue in the campaign...."[21]

Cuomo was at the center of public opinion on this issue. A CBS News election day poll revealed that 58% of New York voters believed that President Reagan's economic program had hurt New York, whereas only 25% believed that it had helped.[22] In addition, a Marist Institute for Public Opinion (MIPO) election analysis found that a voter's view on President Reagan's economic program was the best single indicator of preference for Cuomo or Lehrman. Voters who believed that the Reagan economic program was a good thing for New York State supported Lehrman by 3:1. Conversely, voters who opposed Reaganomics favored Cuomo by 3:1.[23] As in the primary campaign against Koch, Cuomo focused attention on the issue of Reaganomics and demonstrated the importance of national policy to the state's electorate. Cuomo had shaped the political agenda and had successfully articulated his approach.

Another example of the Cuomo Factor is seen in Mario Cuomo's ability to define Democratic Party philosophy and the role of government in a way which is meaningful to today's voters. Cuomo has developed his positions, presented them with consistency, and effectively provided direction for the electorate. Unlike many other Democrats, Cuomo has been able to appeal to a broader audience.

During the 1982 primary against Ed Koch, Cuomo called the contest a battle for the soul of the Democratic Party. He drew a contrast between his view of government and Koch's. According to Cuomo, Koch believed that government was trying to do too much and that more should be left to the private sector and volunteers. Cuomo argued for the need to maintain an important place for government, "we should have *only* the government that we need. But we must insist on *all* the government we need."[24]

Cuomo made his case for continued government involvement in domestic policy in a manner appealing to voters. His use of the "family of New York" slogan provided a vehicle for what amounted to an updated version of traditional values and beliefs. Reflecting upon the campaign, Cuomo wrote, "I needed a new way...to make them listen to what I was saying without concluding that it was somehow out of date...I found it in the idea of 'family.' That concept described as well as it can be described by me the indispensable importance of sharing benefits and burdens, the notion of communal strength and of obligation to the whole."[25]

Using this approach to communicate his concept of government's role, Cuomo succeeded in re-assembling the Democratic coalition when he defeated Koch.[26] Cuomo's appeal to this constituency contrasted with Koch's stand during the campaign. "Slamming the unions and minorities!" charged Cuomo. "Is that a reason to support a *Democrat* for office?"[27] Cuomo's support from labor was especially instrumental to his victory. The state's AFL-CIO and the Civil Service Employees Association provided Cuomo with the personnel necessary to field an impressive campaign organization and contributed to his well executed get-out-the-vote effort on primary day. "In last week's primary," Frank Lynn noted, "thousands of union members worked phone banks and canvassed voters on Mr. Cuomo's behalf. Rarely has a Democratic candidate been perceived as more anti-labor than Mayor Koch—and rarely has labor reacted so strongly."[28] A post-primary analyst noted, "the Cuomo street operation was unlike anything seen in politics here for some time—nearly 10,000 volunteers working phones and banging on doors across the state on primary day seeking Cuomo voters."[29]

In the general election campaign, Cuomo had to defend his support from labor when he was again attacked on the issue of union endorsements. During the *New York Post* debate, Lehrman said "it is the union bosses, not the civil servants, who in fact made Mario Cuomo's campaign go in the primary, and these are the people to whom he is beholden. The very same people who produced the fiscal crisis...Do we want to turn over the state government of New York to the same people who broke the backs of the city in 1974 and 1975?"

Cuomo responded by appealing to progressive values. "...you have revealed one of the most depressing vulnerabilities for new political people. You have given way to the temptation to scapegoat...and I think it's unfortunate. What you just said about...people who make $12,000, $13,000, $15,000, and $17,000 a year, who helped save this city of New York that had been bankrupted by a whole series of people...You're wrong and it's irresponsible...I want to help those people who make $12,000, $15,000, $17,000. The black faces, the brown faces, the white faces, the people who make this city work. They're my people, Lew." Cuomo continued, "I am beholden to three million working people in this state. Who are you beholden to, Lew, the people who gave you money?"[30]

Cuomo discussed the needs of these blue-collar workers without excluding the realities of a changing economy and was able to communicate his position to the general electorate. Cuomo pointed out, "Surely it is wrong to say that 20 years ago we could not have foreseen the coming of obsolescence, the gathering of forces that would humble our outdated efforts. Surely it is even more wrong to say that it is too late now to reindustrialize. We can find ways to restore the old industries...It is not necessary to abandon our old industries in an exhaustive pursuit of new ones. Both can flourish."[31] In this way, Cuomo combined an updated appeal for support with traditional themes.

In the general election campaign against Lew Lehrman, Cuomo's views on government's role were also put to the test. The Cuomo-Lehrman contest developed into a struggle involving how President Reagan's philosophy of limited government had effected New York. Lehrman expressed the view, "There is a fundamental difference between me and my opponent. I am not running for governor because I, like Mario Cuomo, believe I can solve all the problems of New Yorkers. I'm running for governor because I believe the people of New York can solve their problems if we will only release their energies and take the oppressive burden of government off...."[32] Cuomo, in contrast, stressed that government has an obligation "to help those who are in need—people who are in wheelchairs because they are born that way, people who are old, a pregnant woman in Essex County that cannot feed a fetus, a child she is carrying...."[33]

More than any other Democratic candidate in recent years Cuomo emphasized his party's commitment to the plight of the poor and the disabled and to the need for government to address social problems. In a debate sponsored by the *New York*

Post, Cuomo challenged Lehrman, "If you [Lehrman] took a poll that tells you people don't like poor people anymore and maybe you ought to run against welfare and run against poor people, I'll tell you you're wrong because this state is more intelligent and more sensitive than that. You're making a mistake." Cuomo defended Democratic Party policy initiatives as being "a politics that raised up a whole generation...from poverty to middle class. Who is right, Hoover or FDR?"[34] Cuomo queried.

Since his election in 1982, Governor Cuomo has continued to utilize his ability to develop and present his approach as he has shaped political discourse both in New York State and around the nation. Lars-Erik Nelson, Washington bureau chief for the New York *Daily News,* noted, "Cuomo has strength in that he knows exactly who he is and what he believes. He has an inner compass that tells him which way to go."[35] Cuomo has consistently articulated his views on the role of government and has demonstrated how his conception of Democratic Party philosophy is relevant to today's electorate. This approach has led to an expansion in Cuomo's base of support in New York State and has guided his rise to national prominence.

In his Inaugural Address in January 1983, Governor Cuomo spoke of government's role and how public policy should address societal values. "I believe government's basic purpose is to allow those blessed with talent to go as far as they can—on their own merits. But I believe that government also has an obligation to assist those—who for whatever inscrutable reason, have been left out by fate: the homeless, the infirm, the destitute. To help provide those necessary things which, through no fault of their own they cannot provide for themselves."[36] In this address, Governor Cuomo sharpened his approach to government's role by defining it in terms of what he called "progressive pragmatism," a mix of compassion based on the notion of government as a family and common sense given budgetary realities. "I know them well," Cuomo said in discussing the problems he would have to face as governor. "...the deficits, the stagnant economy, the hordes of homeless, unemployed and victimized: the loss of spirit and belief...." Despite an uncertain budget picture, Cuomo pledged to address these societal problems because, "a technically balanced budget that fails to meet the reasonable needs of the middle class and poor would be the emblem of hypocrisy."[37]

Similarly, in his first State-of-the-State message, Cuomo restated his progressive and pragmatic approach to the role of government by appealing to Democratic Party values while being sensitive to budget concerns. "The real challenge before us is to balance our books the way a family would—without abandoning our weak, without sacrificing the future of our young, without destroying the environment that supports us."[38] Cuomo was guided by the desire to present a balanced view. According to his former Secretary Michael Del Guidice, "The budget [submitted by Cuomo] aims at meeting the philosophy that we've got to be very progressive in terms of programs and services, but we've got to be realistic about the economics."[39]

More recently, Cuomo has communicated this approach to government in a national setting and has continued to be a consistent voice for a positive role for government. He entered the national limelight when he gave his keynote address at the Democratic National Convention in the summer of 1984. In that speech, Cuomo incorporated themes from his Inaugural Address of 1983. He spoke of the need for a family approach to government policy. Cuomo stated that government's role and Democratic Party philosophy could be better understood using the metaphor of a covered wagon moving toward the new frontier. The wagon's occupants are members of groups such as Catholics, minorities, women, and the disabled. They are linked because the wagon's journey, in keeping with Democratic Party philosophy, requires more than individual effort.[40] Gerald Pomper, in describing Cuomo's presentation, extended the metaphor, "The world of the frontier is a harsh world. Resources are scarce, so mutual aid is required, to reap crops, raise barns and build schools, pave roads, and care for the poor. For Democrats, these activities require government...."[41]

Cuomo, reflecting his concern for traditional values, recounted the heritage of the Democratic Party. He saw the future of the Democratic Party as being linked to the successes the immigrants and their children enjoyed under earlier Democratic administrations. In so doing, Cuomo's attempt to broaden and update the Democratic Party's appeal was directed to people who, like himself, still identify with the plight of the immigrants even if they no longer experience many of the troubles of the immigrant generation.

Following the convention in 1984, Cuomo has continued to articulate his view of Democratic Party philosophy as a guide to government policy. In his 1985 State-of-the-State message, Cuomo urged, "We have always believed in *only* the government we need...On the other hand, we have always sought balance and reasonableness in everything we do. We have always been able to provide *all* the government we need...The future once happened here. In this building, in this very Assembly Chamber, half a century ago, a generation of men and women defined the legislative agenda that eventually changed all of America—and through America, helped change the world. That agenda became the basis of nearly 50 years of prosperity and opportunity. This is now a whole new era and a whole new opportunity."[42]

Similarly, in a 1985 lecture at Yale University he called on the Democratic Party to reaffirm the principles that have governed the United States for nearly five decades.[43] Cuomo stated that Democrats should retain those principles and should reject any new philosophy in the wake of President Reagan's landslide re-election. "[They] have proven their worth in practice," Cuomo maintained. "...the bottom line is this: programs and policies change; our principles don't."[44]

Cuomo continued to emphasize the need for government to play an important role in domestic policy in an address before the Abraham Lincoln Association in Springfield, Illinois. He noted, "for all our affluence and might, despite what every day is described as our continuing economic recovery, nearly one in every seven Americans lives in poverty...Our identity as a people is hostage to the grim facts of more than 33 million Americans for whom equality and opportunity is not yet an attainable reality...Some people look at these statistics and the suffering people behind them, and deny them, pretending instead we are all one great 'shining city on a hill'...[but] there can be no shining city when one in seven of us is denied the promise of the Declaration."[45]

According to public television's David Hepp, the Springfield address involved the "familiar Cuomo themes—active government and helping the less fortunate. But he struck a new chord here in Springfield, and he hit it right. He started talking about the underclass in America, and he is one of the few politicians who is speaking out about this on a national stage. Cuomo struck them as an original, that he has a sense of direction and a mission. He seems to be speaking out of what he really believes. The other thing he has with the audience is that he can move people with words. He clearly moved the audience."[46] Similarly, David Broder identified Cuomo as one of the Democrats on the national scene who provides for Democrats "a welcome sign that all may not be lost." He notes that Cuomo erases the "widespread belief that the Democrats have lost both their voice and their sense of direction."[47]

Following up the Illinois speech, Cuomo addressed a newspaper publishers' convention in San Francisco. He directed his remarks to the social policies of the Reagan Administration and accused President Reagan of "squandering" billions of dollars on defense while at the same time fostering "the denial of compassion" in social programs.[48]

In the 1986 campaign for governor, Republican Andrew O'Rourke opposed Cuomo's views on government's role by noting that beyond disagreements with Cuomo on specific issues "the telling difference between us is our belief in the proper role for government."[49] In a reference to Cuomo's frequent use of "the family of New York," O'Rourke commented, "I believe that government ought to be like a good relative or close friend—always close at hand, ready to step in when needed or asked, but always sure to knock first."[50] Cuomo saw this election contest as involving a choice for New Yorkers "between two opposing philosophies of government: the deficit-ridden, harsh style we have seen in Washington for the past five years, and the fiscally responsible, progressive government we've practiced here at home."[51]

Cuomo has used both the campaign forum and his Administration to define his positions and establish his role. He has enjoyed extensive popularity in New York State and has come to the forefront of national politics by developing his approach and effectively communicating his views. He has raised issues that extend beyond the borders of New York State and has successfully related these issues to the concerns of the New York electorate. Cuomo represents an unusual combination of progressive values and pragmatic approaches. Through the positions he emphasizes and his ability to communicate a sense of direction to voters, he has become a contemporary politician with great potential for shaping the future of American politics.

New York State voters respond positively to the job Mario

Cuomo is doing as governor. In a MIPO poll conducted in June 1983, Cuomo had the approval of 57.0% of the state's voters.[52] A year later, his rating had risen to 59.0%. In June 1985, 69.6% of the state's voters saw Cuomo as doing either an "excellent" or a "good" job in office. In June 1986, his approval rating was 70.6%. His landslide re-election in which he carried a record-breaking 56 of 62 counties in New York State confirmed his across-the-board appeal.

Survey data reveal that voters see Cuomo as a good leader for New York State, as taking clearly defined positions on issues, as having compassion for the needs of the poor and the elderly, as having policies that are fiscally sound, and as being someone who speaks on behalf of traditional family values. On each of these issues, more than two-thirds of the voters rate Cuomo positively. These responses underscore the point that Cuomo's image is consistent with the themes he highlights.

Not only does the electorate assess Governor Cuomo favorably, but the survey data on Cuomo's popularity suggest that the composition of those who are receptive to his approach is especially significant. Since his election in 1982, Mario Cuomo has established new bridges of support in New York State politics. His popularity extends beyond the traditional Democratic stronghold of New York City, where he received a 72.3% approval rating in a June 1986 MIPO statewide poll, to the suburbs surrounding New York City. In this suburban region of Nassau and Suffolk counties on Long Island, and Westchester and Rockland counties to the north of New York City, Cuomo received a 71.6% approval rating.

These suburban voters have been seen as largely outside the grasp of Democratic candidates electorally. In 1980 and 1984, this four county region, which now accounts for 23% of the state's electorate, contributed to significant GOP landslides. Ronald Reagan carried New York State in 1980 by 165,459 votes. His margin of victory in the four suburban counties was 324,521. In 1984, Reagan carried New York State as a whole by 8%; in these suburbs, his margin was 24.9%. Similarly, in 1980, this same area provided Republican Senator Alfonse D'Amato a margin of 143,552 votes over his opponents. His statewide margin was 80,991 votes. In each of these contests, suburban voters held the balance between victory and defeat.

Because of suburban growth and its increasing importance politically, a candidate for statewide office must make a strong showing in this region. Although Mario Cuomo's appeal to suburban voters developed over time, the Cuomo Factor has found a home in the very communities where voters are thought to be conservative and opposed to government intervention into domestic policy. His appeal to these voters is as surprising as it is significant. In addition to his high popularity rating among Democrats, Cuomo has extensive appeal among large numbers of Independent voters and significant numbers of liberal and moderate Republicans. He is very popular among Protestant and Jewish voters and has been able to reincorporate Catholic voters into the Democratic base of support. Cuomo's message is particularly well received in these suburban communities among professionally employed voters and those with higher levels of education.

Mario Cuomo's popularity is defined, therefore, by the bridge he has built which connects Democratic New York City to the suburbs on the city's rim. The development of the suburbs, the attitudes of its voters, and Governor Cuomo's relationship with this electorate represent the core of the following analysis.

Chapter Two

The Political Development of the New York Suburbs

New York State politics has traditionally focused on the classic rivalry between urban-liberal-Democratic New York City and the rural-conservative-Republican rest of the state. Over the past four decades, however, the New York political scene has evolved into something very different. This transformation has been the result of the development of a third region within the state—the New York suburbs.[1] With the growth of this region and the shrinking electoral power of New York City, the suburbs have assumed a much larger role in New York State politics and represent the key to electoral success in state elections (See Table 2.1).

The emergence of this region as a vital partner in New York State politics is due to several decades of population growth and economic expansion. This pattern of development suggests that two factors have combined to alter the character of today's suburbs. First, large numbers of New York City residents left the city following World War II to establish residence in the suburbs. These migrants diffused the partisan composition of the region. Second, as the population grew, the suburbs underwent an economic transformation and became more self-contained, heterogeneous, and urbanized. This has also contributed to the establishment of new political associations and

---

Table 2.1

Proportion of Registration in Each Region of New York State 1940-1985

	Upstate	New York City	Suburbs
1985	41.1%	35.9%	23.0%
1980	40.8%	36.6%	22.6%
1975	39.2%	39.5%	21.3%
1970	37.5%	41.5%	20.9%
1965	36.9%	44.0%	19.1%
1960	39.4%	42.7%	17.9%
1955	49.9%	31.9%	18.2%
1950	42.8%	43.6%	13.5%
1945	45.5%	42.6%	11.9%
1940	40.7%	48.6%	10.7%

Source: New York State Board of Elections and the New York Red Book. Proportions compiled by MIPO.

---

issue concerns in the area. This chapter focuses on this process of suburbanization.[2]

Since the relationship between suburban living and Republican Party identification was seen as a well established political truth, the post-World War II flight to the suburbs was touted as the Republican answer to the Democratic majority in New York State and nationwide. Kevin Phillips noted, ''new suburbia is turning into a bastion of white conservatism...As in the past, changing population patterns have set the scene for a new political alignment.''[3] The GOP's growing optimism was based on the socioeconomic characteristics of suburbia at the time. As Everett Ladd and Charles Hadley wrote, ''The key ingredient then was deemed to be affluence: the American middle classes had long been decisively Republican, postwar prosperity was expanding dramatically the ranks of the middle class, and the Republican Party would ride growing *embourgeoisement* to national ascendancy."[4]

Several perspectives were advanced about this anticipated change in political party affiliation: the conversion thesis, the transplantation thesis, and a variation. According to the conversion thesis, the exodus from the city to the suburbs in the 1950s would lead to a massive conversion of Democrats to Republicans. As Warren Miller and Teresa Levitin noted, "As Democratic urban dwellers moved to the suburbs and joined the new socioeconomic group of affluent suburbanites, their conversion to the political attitudes and Republican Party support characterizing their new suburban neighbors seemed inevitable."[5] In this view, urban Democrats would change into suburban Republicans as they renounced the city for their new environment. As Frederick Wirt pointed out, "Once tied to the party by occupational, ethnic, and religious bonds, the Democratic affiliation of the *emigré* begins to waver once he signs the mortgage note on his suburban ranch house."[6] The new suburbanite would find the views of the older Republican suburban resident more reasonable, particularly with respect to property rights and tax values. He would leave behind his Democratic past and emulate the politics of the new home area. "So, he winds up voting for Republicans in state and national elections, as the older residents have always done. It is his way of signifying he has left the city behind; more than that, it consolidates his status as a man who is coming up in the world."[7]

The second view of the anticipated Republican expansion in the suburbs is the transplantation thesis. As part of his review of this approach, Robert Wood identified that it was mainly people ripe for political change in the first place who left the city. The already upwardly mobile and middle class in self-image would be more likely to migrate from the city and would readily blend into the existing conservative, Republican suburbs.

23

THE CUOMO FACTOR

A variant of the transplantation perspective suggested that Democrats would be more likely to move to Democratic suburbs, and Republicans would seek out Republican suburbs. They would not undergo conversion or transplantation, but the durability of their partisan attachments would continue. The growth of Republicanism in the suburbs, from this view, would be attributable to the greater propensity for upper-class Republicans to migrate.[8]

Regardless of which thesis was used to describe the motivation and social dynamics associated with postwar suburban development, each perspective concluded that moving to the suburbs involved a process of assimilation or transformation in the social and political identification of the new settlers. In this way, suburban expansion represented an avenue for the eventual dominance of the GOP in New York State and national politics.

These contentions seemed to be easily substantiated. Spurred by an optimistic economic outlook and by a federal government which encouraged economic development, suburban growth throughout the nation took off at an unprecedented rate. In the three decades following World War II, the population in the nation's suburbs nearly tripled. By 1975, suburban political power accounted for the largest bloc of seats in the U.S. House of Representatives. This pattern continued with the reapportionment following the 1980 Census, and by 1984, 45% of the nation's population lived in suburban communities.[9] Examination of growth rates within metropolitan regions reveals the enormous expansion in the suburbs relative to the cities during this period (See Table 2.2a).

The New York suburbs were no exception. From 1940 to 1950, the four county region surrounding New York City increased in population by 32.9% (See Table 2.2b). Nassau and Suffolk counties on Long Island had increases of 65.4% and 39.9%, respectively. Westchester and Rockland counties to the north of New York City also experienced significant growth during the decade, although not as great. Rockland County increased by 20.2% and Westchester County increased by 9.1%.

During the 1950s, these four New York suburban counties experienced even greater population growth. Nassau and Suffolk counties continued to lead in the expansion with population increases of 93.3% and 141.5%. Westchester County grew by 29.2% and Rockland County expanded by 53.2% during the decade. If the New York City suburban counties in Connecticut and New Jersey were included, the population of this suburban region in 1960 actually surpassed that of New York City.

The period from 1960 to 1970 also showed significant expansion in the region, although at a reduced rate of growth. Nassau County grew by 9.9%. Suffolk County increased by 69.0%. Westchester County increased by 10.6% and Rockland County expanded by 68.0%. The region had a total growth rate during this decade of 26.4%, as compared to 75.0% in the previous decade. These suburbs now constituted 20.2% of the entire state population, more than doubling what they had been at the end of World War II. By 1970, both Nassau and Suffolk counties were among the 25 largest counties in population in the country. Had these two suburban counties been a city, they would have been the fourth largest city in the nation.

During the 1970s, there was a stabilization in population growth. Yet, the population within this four county region still increased by 1.4%, despite a statewide decline of 3.7%. Suffolk County had the greatest growth in population within the region during this decade and Rockland County also showed a moderate increase. Westchester and Nassau counties experienced slight declines (See Table 2.2b).

This post-World War II population growth matched the expectations of those who foresaw the suburbs becoming a major

Table 2.2a
Comparison of National Urban and Suburban Growth Rates
Within Metropolitan Areas 1910-1980

	Urban (Inside Central City)	Suburban (Outside Central City)
1970-1980	0.1%	18.2%
1960-1970	5.3%	28.2%
1950-1960	10.7%	48.5%
1940-1950	14.7%	35.9%
1930-1940	5.6%	14.6%
1920-1930	24.3%	32.3%
1910-1920	27.7%	20.0%

Source: U.S. Census of Population, *Characteristics of the Population, Number of Inhabitants,* U.S. Summary for respective years.

Table 2.2b
Percentage of Population Change for the Suburban Counties,
the New York Suburbs, and New York State 1910-1980

	Nassau	Rockland	Suffolk	Westchester	Total Suburbs	NYS	Suburban % of NYS
1970-1980	-7.5	12.9	13.9	-3.1	1.4	-3.7	21.3
1960-1970	9.9	68.1	69.0	10.6	26.4	8.7	20.2
1950-1960	93.3	53.2	141.5	29.3	75.0	13.2	17.4
1940-1950	65.4	20.2	39.9	9.1	32.9	10.0	11.2
1930-1940	34.2	24.6	22.5	10.1	19.8	7.1	9.3
1920-1930	140.3	30.8	46.1	51.2	66.8	21.2	8.3
1910-1920	50.3	-2.8	14.7	21.7	22.8	14.0	6.0

Source: Compiled by MIPO from U.S. Census of Population figures for respective years.

entity in New York State politics. As the massive influx of new voters to these suburban communities swelled the election rolls, statewide elections in New York were no longer contests between upstate and New York City. These suburban voters, as a proportion of the entire state electorate, grew from 10.7% in 1940 to 23.0% in 1985 (See Table 2.3).

Table 2.3
Suburban Proportion of New York State Registration 1940-1985

	New York Suburbs
1985	23.0%
1980	22.6%
1975	21.3%
1970	20.9%
1965	19.1%
1960	17.9%
1955	18.2%
1950	13.5%
1945	11.9%
1940	10.7%

Source: New York State Board of Elections and the New York Red Book. Proportions compiled by MIPO.

The statewide vote for president since the 1930s illustrates the regional shift in electoral strength within the state (See Table 2.4). For example, in the presidential contest of 1932, 9.9% of the statewide vote was cast from this four county region. In 1984, it accounted for 24.2% of the vote. In contrast, the New York City share of the statewide vote fell from 46.8% in 1932 to 32.4% in 1984 (See Table 2.4).

Initially, the population growth in the New York suburbs did benefit the GOP. From 1945 to 1955, Republican Party enrollment in these suburbs jumped by 297,303 registrants while Democratic Party enrollment increased by only 128,360. As expressed by one GOP suburbanite at the time, "When he acquires a house and a piece of land in the suburbs, a voter starts thinking about taxes and tends to become conservative."[10] Hopes for a continued GOP boom were further encouraged by strong Republican Party organizations already in existence in

---

Table 2.4

Regional Proportion of the New York State Vote for President 1932-1984

	Upstate	New York City	Suburbs
1984	43.4%	32.4%	24.2%
1980	44.6%	30.9%	24.4%
1976	43.0%	32.8%	24.2%
1972	40.4%	36.4%	23.2%
1968	39.4%	38.5%	22.1%
1964	38.4%	41.7%	19.9%
1960	39.4%	42.4%	18.2%
1956	38.7%	44.6%	16.6%
1952	38.3%	47.8%	13.9%
1948*	37.7%	51.0%	11.3%
1944	37.0%	52.7%	10.3%
1940	38.6%	51.2%	10.2%
1936	40.5%	49.6%	9.8%
1932	43.3%	46.8%	9.9%

Source: New York State Board of Elections and the New York Red Book. Proportions compiled by MIPO.

*1948 percentages do not include vote for Socialist, Industrial Government and Socialist Worker Candidates.

---

the suburbs. These Republican organizations were primed to expand their power with the infusion of the new settlers from the city. For instance, Nassau County's Republican Party was reminiscent of New York City's Tammany Hall machine. "...GOP workers busily [did] their best to get sewers for householders with flooded new homes, stop lights at crossings where mothers complain[ed] their children [were] unprotected, and paving on new streets."[11]

But the projection that the GOP would dominate American

politics with the growth of the suburbs was not realized. As the region's population grew, the suburbs developed in unanticipated ways. First, despite their new homes and enhanced economic status, which were thought to dictate their political orientation, newcomers did not adopt the conservative views of their environs. They created a diversity of political outlook which diffused the partisan composition of the area. Second, the growth in population led to a major economic expansion which changed the socioeconomic characteristics of the region. As will be discussed, the suburbs became self-contained, heterogeneous, and urbanized.

Population movement is often associated with a modification in the social and economic characteristics of a region. Even relatively limited increases in population are frequently accompanied by substantial social and economic alterations. Along with change of this sort, shifts in regional politics and voting patterns can occur.[12] Ladd and Hadley have discussed the interrelatedness of these various aspects of socioeconomic change. They observed, "Many of the components of change are not directly political, and most, surely do not originate in the polity: they encompass the economy, lifestyles, culture, values, virtually the entire sweep of societal interactions. But collectively, these transformations define a new environment for political life."[13]

This process of suburbanization, involving new people and a new socioeconomic base, changed the politics of the region. Enrollment data since the mid-1950s indicate that the proportion of Republicans in the suburbs fell off dramatically. Despite an overall increase of 276,578 registered Republicans from 1955 to 1984, the Republican proportion of the suburban electorate declined by 23.3% (See Table 2.5). With this decline, it became apparent that the suburbs were not developing into a homogeneous Republican monolith. These voters were not nearly so

Republican as the older suburbanites and were not so easily converted to Republicanism.[14] The belief in Republican dominance in the region had rested on erroneous assumptions involving the character of the middle class, which was seen as remaining largely unchanged while its numbers increased. Furthermore, the Democratic appeal of the 1930s was thought to be unacceptable to those people experiencing increased affluence.[15] There is no evidence that Democratic oriented voters switched parties because they moved from the cities to the suburbs or became more affluent. As Ladd and Hadley discussed the dynamics of the period, "The socioeconomic structure of the Democratic coalition changed substantially as important segments of its membership rode the wave of growing prosperity, and as the party's programs and policies became securely fixed as compatible with the needs and aspirations of much of the new middle class."[16] The old affluent were traditionally Republican. The new suburbanite was neither so affluent nor so Republican.[17]

This dilution of Republican Party strength was partially due to the greater Democratic affiliation of those who migrated from New York City. For example, the party identification of present-day suburbanites who had once resided in New York City is 31.4% Democratic and 28.9% Republican, compared with 20.5% Democratic and 38.2% Republican for suburban residents who had never lived in the city. Despite this migration, however, the Democratic Party did not command suburban electoral politics. The proportion of enrolled suburban Democrats increased by only 6.7% during this thirty year period (See Table 2.5).

What accounted for the greatest proportion of the changing electorate was the number of voters who chose not to enroll in any political party: the Independents. The percentage of registered Independent voters increased from a mere 9.0% in 1955 to 23.1% of the electorate in 1984 (See Table 2.5). The trend toward party independence is consistent throughout the region generally and is comparable among current suburbanites who once lived in New York City and suburban residents who never lived in New York City. The figures are 39.7% and 41.3%, respectively.

Table 2.5
Party Enrollment in the New York Suburbs 1955-1984

	Democrat	**Republican**	**Independent**	**Other**
1984	32.2%	41.7%	23.1%	3.0%
1983	32.7%	42.4%	21.7%	3.2%
1982	32.6%	42.6%	21.6%	3.1%
1981	32.4%	43.1%	21.3%	3.2%
1980	32.9%	42.8%	21.1%	3.2%
1979	34.2%	44.7%	17.8%	3.2%
1978	34.5%	45.3%	17.1%	3.1%
1977	34.9%	44.5%	17.5%	3.2%
1976	34.8%	44.3%	17.7%	3.2%
1975	34.8%	48.2%	13.5%	3.4%
1974	34.6%	48.5%	13.4%	3.4%
1973	34.2%	48.1%	14.0%	3.7%
1972	34.3%	47.3%	14.6%	3.8%
1971	34.9%	47.5%	13.9%	3.7%
1970	33.7%	49.5%	13.6%	3.3%
1969	33.4%	50.2%	13.6%	2.9%
1968	33.2%	50.4%	13.6%	2.8%
1967	33.6%	51.7%	12.7%	2.1%
1966	33.5%	52.4%	12.5%	1.6%
1965	33.8%	52.5%	12.5%	1.1%
1964	33.6%	52.8%	12.6%	1.0%
1963	30.6%	57.2%	11.4%	0.8%
1962	30.0%	58.0%	11.4%	0.6%
1961	29.8%	58.2%	11.3%	0.7%
1960	29.3%	58.3%	11.7%	0.7%
1959	27.3%	61.2%	11.0%	0.6%
1958	26.8%	61.6%	11.0%	0.6%
1957	26.4%	63.2%	10.0%	0.5%
1956	25.1%	64.6%	9.9%	0.5%
1955	25.5%	65.0%	9.0%	0.4%

Source: New York State Board of Elections and the New York Red Book. Proportions compiled by MIPO.

THE CUOMO FACTOR

The increase in Independent voters represents the most significant development in suburban politics. Morris Janowitz has pointed out that one of the major trends in American politics has been "the gradual but persistent increase in the proportion of the electorate who consider themselves to be Independents."[18] Suburbanites, although conscientious about registering to vote, have increasingly chosen not to enroll in any political party.

The rise in the number of Independents deprived either political party from controlling the region. The politics which subsequently developed resembled neither the Republicanism of the old suburbs nor the Democratic Party politics of the urban neighborhoods in New York City. Instead, the changed electorate created a new suburban politics with its own distinct character. For many new residents, the growth of suburbia not only meant a change in lifestyle, but a distancing from old style party politics. The existing political party organizations did not flourish with the expansion in population. As David Broder commented, "The mobility—both geographic and social—of postwar Americans tended to make associative politics harder to sustain."[19] As noted in *Fortune,* "Party machines of the old type, which still [had] some effectiveness in city wards and rural counties, simply [would] not work in most suburbs. Association of candidates with the style and practices of the 'old politics' [carried] a heavy negative charge in the minds of suburban voters."[20] The new suburbanite with his rising socioeconomic status saw himself as able to make discriminatory choices without the assistance of traditional party organizations.

The voters' political independence directed party activity away from that associated with traditional party organizations and forced candidates to develop new means to communicate with voters. By the late 1960s, candidates were increasingly utilizing campaign management firms in the suburbs. These were first used in West Coast communities which lacked traditional forms of political party organization and fit nicely into the relatively organizationless politics of the suburbs. Accompanying this changed politics were efforts on behalf of candidates in the suburbs to rely on television as the means to reach the electorate. The suburban arena was well suited to this media. As A. James Reichley pointed out, "The physical, as well as social, nature of the suburbs [made] TV a particularly necessary political tool. Lacking well-defined civic centers or downtowns, suburban communities provid[ed] candidates with few natural forums. Scattered over thousands of acres, they [made] old-fashioned personal campaigning too time consuming to be productive."[21]

Today's suburbs reflect this changed composition of partisanship and this new style of non-party politics. But the process of suburbanization not only facilitated independent politics, it provided these communities with an opportunity to develop their economic independence, as well. As more employment opportunities became based in the area and commuting to the central city slackened, the character of the region changed from bedroom communities of the central city to self-contained, heterogeneous, and urbanized suburbs. As will be discussed in Chapters Three and Four, this change in the characteristics of the region, although gradual, has had a significant impact on the development of the area: the issues it has had to confront and the political views of its citizenry.

Despite the growth in suburban population following World War II, employment initially remained largely in New York City, and the labor force commuted from the suburbs to the city for work. The relative homogeneity of the region was thus maintained in the short run. But new residents were not the only ones being lured into these suburban communities. Industrial relocation and expansion in the suburbs paralleled the burgeoning growth in population. As *The New York Times* observed, "One distinguishing feature of postwar growth in the suburbs is the extent to which business and industry have also taken to the country."[22]

In tracing this pattern of economic growth, a study by the Regional Plan Association found that by the mid-1950s, "More than four-fifths of the postwar economic expansion in the New York metropolitan area went to the 17 counties of the city's environs and less than one-fifth occurred within the city." The four New York suburban counties alone "got 38% of the increase, though they had held only 7% of the total in 1946."[23] Industrial employment in Nassau and Suffolk counties, for example, increased by 103.6% between 1946 and 1952, as compared to the national average of 12.1%.[24] Although the entire New York area lost about 600,000 jobs in the 1970s, 60% of the manufacturing jobs that New York City lost wound up in its suburbs.[25]

With the dispersal of jobs, the suburbs became more economically independent. As Peter Muller has pointed out, there has been an "intensified intrametropolitan deconcentration of economic activity that has been under way since the mid-1960s, a movement following in the wake of the massive population exodus from the central cities during the two preceding decades."[26] The region has exhibited greater diversity in its industrial and occupational job mix. A description of employment opportunities in the suburbs includes the remaining manufacturing industry, extensive high tech expansion, and developing service jobs. Such diversity has resulted in the ability of many suburban communities to revitalize their own economies and to minimize the impact of downturns in the national economy even during recent recessions (See Table 2.6).

Economic expansion and diversity exist throughout New York's suburbs. For example, the mix of economic activity from Great Neck to Montauk Point has provided Long Island with

Table 2.6

Annual Average Unemployment Rate for Suburban Counties,
New York State, and United States 1979-1984*

	Nassau	Rockland	Suffolk	Westchester	New York State	United States
1984	4.9%	4.8%	5.4%	4.3%	7.2%	7.5%
1983	6.1%	6.2%	6.9%	5.6%	8.6%	9.6%
1982	6.0%	5.7%	6.7%	5.3%	8.6%	9.7%
1981	5.5%	5.6%	6.3%	4.7%	7.6%	7.6%
1980	5.6%	5.1%	6.3%	4.4%	7.5%	7.1%
1979	6.3%	5.1%	6.2%	4.6%	7.1%	5.8%

Source: State of New York Department of Labor BLMI Report No. 2 FY 1986.
*Not seasonally adjusted.

the resilience that has eluded many other areas. The growth in manufacturing jobs in the 1980s was almost 15% over the previous decade. This expansion occurred while New York State was suffering an 18% loss. Meanwhile, there was an even greater gap in the growth of non-manufacturing jobs in Nassau and Suffolk counties as compared with the rest of the state. The expansion in the suburbs occurred in finance, insurance, real estate, and services and trade industries (See Table 2.7).

In Westchester and Rockland counties, a similar economic diversity emerged. In Westchester County manufacturing remained an important, though reduced, proportion of the local economy. Although many manufacturing firms closed or relocated during the recessions in the 1970s, 20% of the jobs in Westchester County remained in firms whose primary activity was manufacturing. The major expansion in the county, however, has been in the trade and service sectors, largely white-collar areas, which account for over half the increase in

Table 2.7

Employment Growth Rates by Industry for Nassau-Suffolk Area,
New York State, and the United States
Three-Year Average 1970-1972 to Three-Year Average 1981-1983

Industrial Sector	Nassau-Suffolk	New York State	United States
Non-agricultural employment, total	+28.9	+ 2.9	+25.5
Manufacturing, total	+14.8	−18.2	+ 0.1
Non-manufacturing, total	+32.4	+ 9.5	+34.3
Construction	−2.9	−19.3	+ 7.7
Transportation, communication, and utilities	+23.0	−12.8	+12.2
Wholesale and retail trade	+26.6	+ 2.6	+32.6
Finance, insurance, real estate	+52.9	+13.5	+42.1
Services and miscellaneous non-manufacturing	+65.3	+32.1	+61.9
Government	+17.8	+ 5.0	+22.7

Source: *County Profiles: Socio-Economic Characteristics, Suffolk County,* New York
State Department of Labor Division of Research and Statistics, October 1984,
pg. 17.

employment in the county since the mid-1970s. Proximity to New York City attracted scores of administrative and sales offices to Westchester County. Rockland County's economy has undergone a similar change. Over the past twenty years, non-manufacturing employment within the county has nearly tripled, dropping manufacturing's share of total employment from 32% in 1961 to 19% in 1981.[27]

The increased location of jobs in the suburbs, along with the combination of manufacturing and non-manufacturing employment, has caused the region to evolve, like other suburbs around the nation, from "an amorphous, bedroom community status to an organized economy clustered around recognizable employment centers drawing on fairly close commuting sheds...."[28] Reflecting these national trends, where more than 70% of suburban residents in the largest metropolitan areas now work in the suburbs, a 1980 poll by *The New York Times* revealed that only 20% of the New York suburban workforce commuted to the city.[29] Although New York City still provides the most centralized economic activity in the area, the percentage of metropolitan area residents working in the city declined from 48% to 42.7% of the total workforce during the 1970s.

Commuting patterns within the New York City metropolitan area also illustrate this change. During that decade, there was a 40.8% rise in the number of area residents employed in Suffolk County. Similarly, the growth in employment opportunities in Westchester County substantially increased the number of area residents working in that county.[30] In addition to the many workers who no longer commute to the city for employment, a growing number of workers now commute between the different suburban counties as job opportunities shift. In the past decade, there has been a 44% increase, for example, in the number of Nassau County residents commuting to jobs in Suffolk County.[31]

As the region has expanded economically and fewer people commute to the central city for employment, the suburbs have become self-sufficient entities, complete with their own economic and cultural activities. The area is no longer an appendage of the central city.[32] As has been noted, "the residents of the [suburban] ring around New York City, once regarded simply as a bedroom for commuters, no longer feel themselves subordinate to New York. The suburbs have become a multi-centered urban chain with surprisingly limited ties to the metropolitan core...Suburban residents have established their own institutions and go about their lives in an increasingly separate world."[33] The greater self-containment of the suburbs is reflected in people's social activities, as well. Less than one-fourth of suburban residents believe that events in the city have a major impact on their lives, and less than one-half indicate that they spend a day or evening in the city at least five times a year.[34]

Louis Masotti and Jeffrey Hadden were among the first to identify this urbanization of the suburbs. Writing in the mid-1970s, they described this concept as the growing economic, cultural, and political independence of the region from the central city. No longer are the suburbs predominantly rural, homogeneous, or characterized by growth solely in newer high tech industries.[35] The realities of this area negate the stereotype of suburban society as characterized by "a complex of purportedly universal attributes: suburbanites [comprising] a homogeneous middle-class population of white-collar central city commuters residing in split-level 'little boxes'...."[36] Today's suburbia is best characterized as a "kaleidoscope of diverse income, ethnic, and lifestyle groups."[37]

Census data on the population characteristics of the region further substantiate the diversity of today's suburbia. The data point to the extensive variety of people within the region and its economic vitality. The suburbs have a varied population, but one with a higher level of income, education, and occupational status as compared to other regions within the state. In terms of income, for example, the suburban population is diverse, but is relatively well off (See Table 2.8a). The suburban population also has a variety of educational backgrounds, but a greater proportion of residents with higher levels of education. Employment in the region is characterized by a large number of professional/managerial members of the workforce (See Table 2.8a). Although the suburban electorate as a whole possesses high socioeconomic characteristics, the migrants from

Table 2.8a

Combined Family Income, Educational Attainment,* and Occupation for the
New York Suburbs and the Rest of New York State

	Nassau	Rockland	Suffolk	Westchester	Total Suburbs	Rest of NYS
Income						
Under $5,000	2.7%	3.2%	3.6%	4.2%	3.4%	9.5%
$5,000-$9,000	5.9%	6.4%	8.6%	7.8%	7.3%	14.5%
$10,000-$14,000	8.1%	8.2%	10.7%	9.7%	9.4%	15.3%
$15,000-$24,000	24.0%	23.4%	29.4%	23.0%	25.5%	28.9%
$25,000-$34,000	24.2%	25.1%	24.6%	20.4%	23.5%	17.6%
$35,000-$49,000	19.9%	21.4%	15.5%	17.5%	18.0%	9.5%
$50,000 or More	15.1%	12.3%	7.5%	17.5%	13.0%	4.7%
Education						
High School	37.7%	33.4%	39.6%	32.2%	36.7%	33.4%
Some College	16.4%	17.4%	16.3%	15.0%	16.1%	13.8%
College	11.5%	11.8%	8.2%	13.0%	10.8%	7.9%
Post-College	12.1%	14.0%	9.6%	14.9%	12.1%	8.7%
Occupation						
Executives, Administrators, Managers	14.8%	13.7%	11.4%	15.2%	13.8%	10.3%
Professional	15.3%	17.6%	14.3%	18.0%	15.8%	14.2%
Technicians (Related-Support)	2.3%	2.8%	3.1%	2.9%	2.8%	2.9%
Support (including Clerical & Sales)	34.8%	29.6%	29.2%	31.6%	31.9%	30.3%
Service Workers	11.2%	14.4%	13.3%	12.3%	12.4%	14.3%
Farming, Forestry, Fishing	0.8%	0.6%	1.4%	0.8%	1.0%	1.4%
Craftsmen	10.5%	10.5%	13.5%	9.2%	11.1%	10.2%
Operatives, Transportation, Material Handling Laborers	10.2%	10.8%	13.9%	9.9%	11.3%	16.3%

Source: Compiled by MIPO from the 1980 Census of Population, *General Social and
 Economic Characteristics, New York.*
*Educational Attainment of Persons 25 Years and Over.

THE CUOMO FACTOR

New York City, who comprise 50.2% of the present suburban
electorate, have particularly high income and employment
status and greater representation at the highest educational
levels (See Table 2.8b).

Table 2.8b

Former New York City Residents vs. Non-New York City Residents by
Income, Education, and Occupation in the New York Suburbs

	Resided in New York City	Never Resided in New York City
Income		
Under $10,000	42.4%	57.6%
$10,000-$24,000	42.4%	57.6%
$25,000-$40,000	45.2%	54.8%
$41,000-$60,000	51.4%	48.6%
over $60,000	64.8%	35.2%
Education		
Less than High School	48.7%	51.3%
High School	46.4%	53.6%
Some College	44.7%	55.3%
College	46.8%	53.2%
Grad/Professional	65.6%	34.4%
Occupation		
Manual	42.6%	57.4%
Clerical/Sales	46.1%	53.9%
Managerial	50.4%	49.6%
Professional	59.1%	40.9%

The development of the suburbs constituted what has been
characterized as a social revolution on wheels. Waves of people
left the central city to settle in the suburbs, and subsequently,
the economic infrastructure of the region has undergone a major

transformation. The net result of this process of suburbanization has been the evolution of a region with a new and distinct political character which has provided the opportunity for a new type of political appeal.

Chapter Three

Contemporary New York Suburban Political Attitudes

The political fabric of today's suburbia reflects the changes which these communities have undergone in their population, in their living environs, and in their issue concerns. The suburban electorate is presently characterized by voters who have shown a decline in partisanship, a high interest in following politics, and a concern for issues in public affairs.[1] Of these factors, the most striking political trend in the region has been the weakening of the partisan attachments of the electorate. This erosion is evidenced by the increase in the number of Independents, by the weakened political attachments of party identifiers, and by the rise in split-ticket voting.

As noted in Chapter Two, the proportion of Independents to enrolled Democrats and Republicans in the suburbs has increased dramatically over recent decades. Independents currently represent 23.1% of registered voters, up from 9.9% in 1956. This decline in party enrollment has been consistently greater in the suburbs than in the rest of New York State (See Table 3.1).

Survey data reveal that the decline in partisanship is even more pervasive than these enrollment figures alone suggest. Comparisons between party enrollment and party identification show that, even among voters who are enrolled in a political party,

Table 3.1
New York State Party Enrollment by Region 1956-1984

	Democrat	Republican	Independent	Other
1984				
Upstate	36.4%	42.4%	18.7%	2.6%
NYC	70.2%	13.0%	15.0%	1.8%
Suburbs	32.2%	41.7%	23.1%	3.0%
1982				
Upstate	35.6%	43.7%	18.3%	2.5%
NYC	70.7%	13.4%	13.5%	2.3%
Suburbs	32.6%	42.6%	21.6%	3.1%
1980				
Upstate	35.3%	44.9%	17.5%	2.4%
NYC	70.1%	13.9%	13.5%	2.5%
Suburbs	32.9%	42.8%	21.1%	3.2%
1978				
Upstate	36.3%	47.7%	13.7%	2.3%
NYC	71.9%	14.5%	10.9%	2.8%
Suburbs	34.5%	45.3%	17.1%	3.1%
1976				
Upstate	36.6%	47.7%	13.2%	2.5%
NYC	69.9%	15.6%	11.3%	3.2%
Suburbs	34.8%	44.3%	17.7%	3.2%
1974				
Upstate	35.5%	51.3%	10.9%	2.3%
NYC	70.1%	17.7%	8.3%	4.0%
Suburbs	34.6%	48.5%	13.4%	3.4%
1972				
Upstate	35.4%	51.3%	10.9%	2.3%
NYC	68.2%	18.1%	9.2%	4.5%
Suburbs	34.3%	47.3%	14.6%	3.8%
1970				
Upstate	34.1%	54.7%	9.5%	1.7%
NYC	68.2%	19.4%	8.0%	4.5%
Suburbs	33.7%	49.5%	13.6%	3.3%
1968				
Upstate	34.3%	55.1%	9.2%	1.5%
NYC	68.7%	20.2%	7.4%	3.7%
Suburbs	33.2%	50.4%	13.6%	2.8%
1966				
Upstate	35.1%	55.1%	8.6%	1.1%
NYC	70.5%	19.9%	6.9%	2.8%
Suburbs	33.5%	52.4%	12.5%	1.6%

Table 3.1 Continued

	Democrat	Republican	Independent	Other
1964				
Upstate	36.8%	54.0%	8.4%	0.8%
NYC	70.4%	20.6%	6.9%	2.2%
Suburbs	33.6%	52.8%	12.6%	1.0%
1962				
Upstate	32.6%	58.7%	8.1%	0.5%
NYC	68.1%	23.5%	6.3%	2.0%
Suburbs	30.0%	58.0%	11.4%	0.6%
1960				
Upstate	33.0%	58.5%	7.9%	0.5%
NYC	67.6%	23.9%	6.3%	2.1%
Suburbs	29.3%	58.3%	11.7%	0.7%
1958				
Upstate	31.3%	60.4%	7.8%	0.4%
NYC	68.8%	22.8%	6.1%	2.3%
Suburbs	26.8%	61.6%	11.0%	0.6%
1956				
Upstate	29.0%	62.9%	7.7%	0.3%
NYC	63.4%	28.0%	6.5%	2.0%
Suburbs	25.1%	64.6%	9.9%	0.5%

Source: New York State Board of Elections and the New York Red Book. Proportions
compiled by MIPO.

Independent identification is prevalent. Although the party
enrollment in the suburbs is reported as 31.2% Democratic, 43.4%
Republican, and 21.2% Independent, voters express their party
identification as 25.3% Democratic, 32.9% Republican, and
39.8% Independent. Independent identification is almost twice
the Independent enrollment (See Table 3.2). In addition, the
majority of voters who identify with either the Democratic or
Republican parties do not see themselves as strongly committed
to that party (See Table 3.2).

Despite the weakened partisanship in the suburbs, these voters
maintain both a high interest in public affairs and a significant
concern for issues in politics. First, the loosening of political party
moorings associated with the rise in Independents has not

45

Table 3.2
New York Suburban Respondent's Party Registration,
Party Identification, and Strength of Partisanship

Party Registration*

"Are you currently registered to vote as a Democrat, Republican, Independent,
Conservative, or Liberal?"

Democrat	31.2%
Republican	43.4%
Independent	21.2%
Conservative	2.4%
Liberal	1.2%
Other	0.7%

Party Identification

"Do you consider yourself to be a Democrat, a Republican, or an Independent?"

Democrat	25.3%
Republican	32.9%
Independent	39.8%
Other	1.9%

Strength of Party Identification**

"Do you consider yourself to be a strong Democrat/Republican or
not a very strong Democrat/Republican?"

	Strong	**Weak**	**Unsure**
Democrat	44.7%	51.2%	4.1%
Republican	39.6%	55.0%	5.4%

*Note: These survey estimates are consistent with the enrollment figures compiled by
the New York State Board of Elections. Their 1986 enrollment figures, collected in the fall of 1985, were: 31.9% Democrat, 42.2% Republican, 22.9% Independent, 2.1% Conservative, 0.6% Liberal, 0.4% Right to Life.
**Asked only of Democrats and Republicans.

resulted in a reduced interest in politics among the region's voters. 72.0% of the suburban electorate indicate that they follow politics either "very closely" or "closely" (See Table 3.3). Suburban voters with higher levels of education are more likely to follow politics, with those at the highest educational levels most likely to do so. 86.5% of voters who have gone beyond college indicate that they follow politics "very closely" or "closely." For voters who have a college degree, 77.6% indicate that they are attentive to politics. For voters who have gone beyond high school but have not finished college, those who have a high school diploma, and those with less than a high school education, the interest in following politics either "very closely" or "closely" is 72.5%, 61.4%, and 53.9%, respectively (See Table 3.3).

Table 3.3

New York Suburban Respondent's Interest in Politics and
Level of Education, Occupation, and Income

"In general, would you say that you follow politics very closely, closely, not very closely or not at all?"

	Closely (1 & 2)	Not Closely (3 & 4)
New York Suburbs*	72.0%	27.9%
Education		
Less than High School	53.9%	46.1%
High School	61.4%	38.6%
Some College	72.5%	27.5%
College	77.6%	22.4%
Grad/Professional	86.5%	13.5%
Occupation		
Manual	64.9%	35.1%
Clerical/Sales	69.0%	31.0%
Managerial	81.5%	18.5%
Professional	82.9%	17.1%
Income		
Under $10,000	51.4%	48.6%
$10,000-$24,000	62.0%	38.0%
$25,000-$40,000	70.1%	29.9%
$41,000-$60,000	77.6%	22.4%
Over $60,000	82.2%	17.8%

*The frequencies for each of the four categories were: 15.1% very closely, 56.9% closely, 24.9% not very closely, and 3.0% not at all.

A similar pattern exists when the occupational status of the voter is analyzed. Professional and managerial members of the workforce are most likely to follow politics. The income level of the voter is another indicator of one's attentiveness to politics. The higher the income of the voter, the more likely he or she is to follow politics. The relationship between education, occupation, and income, and a voter's interest in following politics, is particularly important because of the large number of voters with relatively high levels of education, occupational status, and income in the region. The distinctive political fabric of the suburbs is shaped by this pattern (See Table 3.3).

Second, the suburban electorate is also characterized by the concern individuals place on issues when assessing candidates. Close to half of this electorate stresses the importance of issues in arriving at their candidate choices. This does not mean that these voters rigorously sift through the candidates seeking office, identify those candidates whose positions most closely match their own views, and then automatically vote for those office-seekers. Rather, these voters place a high value on the importance of issues in politics and respond to issue oriented political appeals (See Table 3.4).

The distinctive socioeconomic characteristics of the population help explain the emphasis on issues within the region. For example, the greater the educational level of the suburban voter, the more likely issues are considered the primary factor in assessing a candidate for public office. 58.6% of suburbanites who have a graduate or professional education rank issues as the number one factor; 50.7% of those with a college education consider issues to be most important; 41.5% with some college education value issues the most; 43.4% of high school educated and 28.7% of those with less than a high school education emphasize issues in arriving at their electoral choices (See Table 3.4). Similarly, those members of the workforce who are professionally employed or who are in managerial positions place a high value on issues in assessing candidates. The income level of the voter does not reveal a consistent pattern.

Table 3.4

Most Important Factor in Assessing Candidates and the Respondent's Level of Education, Occupation, and Income in the New York Suburbs

"Of the following, which one do you consider to be the single most important factor in choosing a candidate for office? One, his leadership abilities; two, the political party he represents; three, his experience; or four, his stands on the issues?"

	Leadership	Party	Experience	Issues	Other	Unsure
New York Suburbs	29.4%	2.9%	17.7%	46.4%	2.3%	1.3%
Education						
Less than High School	33.9%	8.5%	22.3%	28.7%	5.1%	1.5%
High School	28.7%	3.1%	22.4%	43.4%	1.2%	1.2%
Some College	31.3%	3.4%	18.5%	41.5%	3.5%	1.8%
College	28.5%	1.9%	17.0%	50.7%	1.4%	0.4%
Grad/Professional	29.0%	1.1%	8.4%	58.6%	2.3%	0.6%
Occupation						
Manual	36.1%	3.1%	15.6%	42.0%	2.7%	0.6%
Clerical/Sales	30.1%	4.5%	17.6%	44.0%	3.3%	0.5%
Managerial	33.3%	2.7%	9.0%	52.3%	2.7%	0.0%
Professional	25.3%	2.1%	16.6%	51.1%	3.0%	1.7%
Income						
Under $10,000	36.0%	6.9%	33.2%	19.4%	0.0%	4.6%
$10,000-$24,000	25.3%	3.4%	21.4%	46.6%	1.7%	1.5%
$25,000-$40,000	32.8%	3.8%	15.3%	43.2%	3.0%	1.8%
$41,000-$60,000	27.2%	1.0%	13.3%	57.0%	1.0%	0.4%
Over $60,000	31.9%	3.6%	12.5%	48.5%	2.9%	0.6%

This discussion about the suburban electorate's interest in following politics and concern for issues when assessing candidates is reinforced by the large number of Independent voters in the region. Prior to the recent growth in Independent identification, political Independents were largely seen as having the weakest ties to the political system as exhibited by a lack of interest and knowledge about politics. Independent identification and the decrease in voting, for example, were thought to go hand in hand. The classic study of voting behavior, *The American Voter,* described this phenomenon as it existed in 1960. "Far from being more attentive, interested, and informed, Independents tend as a group to be somewhat less involved in politics. They have somewhat poorer knowledge of the issues, their image of the candidates is fainter, their interest in the campaign is less, their concern over the outcome is relatively slight, and their choice between competing candidates...seems much less to spring from discoverable evaluations of the elements of national politics."[2]

Today's Independent voter requires re-examination of these assertions. A new Independent voter has emerged with social characteristics and political concerns which differ greatly from the traditional view. Walter Dean Burnham wrote, "Not only the increase but the absolute proportion of Independents has become increasingly identified with the comfortable urban-suburban middle class...A new breed of Independent seems to be emerging as well—a person with a better-than-average education, making a better-than-average income in a better-than-average occupation...."[3]

Voters who see themselves as politically Independent represent close to 40% of today's electorate in the New York suburbs. This voter does not exhibit relatively less interest in politics. Survey results point to comparable figures among Independents, Democrats, and Republicans regarding their interest in politics. Voters who follow politics either "very closely" or "closely" account for 74.2% of the Democrats and 70.5% of the Republicans. 70.8% of the Independents also express a high interest in following politics. Furthermore, these Independent voters are more attentive to politics than either weak partisan Democrats or weak partisan Republicans (See Table 3.5).

Table 3.5
Party Identification and the Respondent's Interest in
Politics in the New York Suburbs

"In general, would you say that you follow politics very closely, closely, not very closely, or not at all?"

	Closely	**Not Closely**
	(1 & 2)	**(3 & 4)**
Democrat	74.2%	25.8%
Strong	82.5%	17.5%
Weak	66.5%	33.5%
Republican	70.5%	29.5%
Strong	82.8%	17.2%
Weak	61.4%	38.6%
Independent	70.8%	29.2%

In addition, these new Independents do not conform to the traditional view concerning the value they place on issues in politics. As Paul Abramson wrote, "Some political scientists have argued that the decline of party loyalties is also related to other trends in American political attitudes and behaviors, such as the tendency of voters to become more politically sophisticated, to think more systematically about political issues...."[4] Independent voters are not turned off to political discourse on issues. Rather than being an uninvolved, uninterested segment of the electorate, these voters bring a selectivity to politics and a high awareness about issues and candidates seeking office. Their concern for issues approximates that held by Democrats and Republicans (See Table 3.6).

Table 3.6

Most Important Factor in Assessing Candidates and the Respondent's Party Identification in the New York Suburbs

"Of the following, which one do you consider to be the single most important factor in choosing a candidate for office? One, his leadership abilities; two, the political party he represents; three, his experience; or four, his stands on the issues."

	Leadership	Party	Experience	Issues	Other	Unsure
Democrat	25.6%	2.7%	17.4%	50.9%	1.6%	1.9%
Republican	30.8%	4.9%	17.5%	42.6%	2.4%	1.7%
Independent	30.8%	1.8%	17.6%	46.7%	2.4%	0.7%

Since these voters are not committed to any political party, the cord linking them to the political process is highly elastic. Unlike strong partisan identifiers, they respond more to short-term issues and the candidates of each election.[5] The weakened partisan attachments of Independents contribute to considerable unpredictability in elections. William Crotty commented, "The Independent voter is up for grabs. It has no allegiances. Its volatility and malleability does little to ease the concern of those who value stability and order in American politics...The Independent vote is fluid. The intensity of its support tends to drift from one candidate and party to the other...."[6] These voters reject the notion that they can do no more than vote straight-ticket Republican or Democratic. As a result, the trend toward split-ticket voting is marked.

The New York suburban electorate, as a whole, is characterized, therefore, by the socioeconomic makeup of the populace, its large number of Independents, and the ties of its voters to the political process. The region's voters show a decline in partisanship, a high interest in following politics, and a concern for issues in their political evaluations. As a result, this electorate displays a high selectivity in voting.

The suburbs now constitute the swing area in New York State politics, and it is a region whose electoral bounty is up for grabs. As enrollment patterns weakened what had been overwhelming Republican strength, electoral competition has increased. In 1964, *The New York Times* chronicled that the political organization and leadership in the suburbs had changed with the fragmentation of power. "The diffusion and dilution of power, politically and economically, that has come into the suburbs [involves] the evolution of a predominantly rural and residential society into one increasingly urban...And because of an increasingly sophisticated, independent electorate, suburban government today is more democratically based than ever before...The Republican monopoly on suburban votes is declining."[7]

From World War II to the 1960s, for example, Republicans held all of the congressional seats in the area. But beginning in the 1960s, the dominance of GOP candidates in congressional elections subsided, and the suburbs began to elect more Democrats to the House. Since then, the number of seats held by Democrats and Republicans has remained fairly even.[8] During the 1960s, Democrats also made substantial inroads in the New York State Assembly. From 1940 to 1960, no Democrat was elected from the suburbs to the Assembly. Since that time, Democrats have generally held between one-quarter and one-third of the seats from the region. Democrats have been less successful, however, in electing representatives to the New York State Senate, where Republicans maintain their command of these offices.

Regarding the U.S. Senate, Republicans have generally carried the region. However, Daniel Patrick Moynihan outpolled what other Democrats have been able to garner. He received 50.1% of the suburban vote in 1976 and 58.6% in 1982. At the gubernatorial level, Democrats have performed better in the suburbs relative to their statewide tally. For example, in 1946 the suburban total for the Democratic candidate for governor was 19.8% less than the Democratic candidate's statewide tally. In 1966 this difference was 10.7%, and by 1986 the gap had closed to 4.7%. In addition, Hugh Carey in 1974 was the first Democratic candidate for governor to win the suburban region in over 50 years, when he received 50.9% of the vote. But Mario Cuomo improved this standing in 1986. His victory represented the highest total in the region for a Democratic gubernatorial candidate in modern political history (See Table 3.7).

Table 3.7
New York Suburban Vote for Governor 1924-1986*

	Democratic Candidate		Republican Candidate	
1986	Cuomo	62.1%	O'Rourke	37.9%
1982	Cuomo	48.2%	Lehrman	51.8%
1978	Carey	46.5%	Wilson	53.5%
1974	Carey	50.9%	Wilson	49.1%
1970	Goldberg	36.1%	Rockefeller	63.9%
1966	O'Connor	35.4%	Rockefeller	64.6%
1962	Morgenthau	34.0%	Rockefeller	66.0%
1958	Harriman	34.6%	Rockefeller	65.4%
1954	Harriman	35.2%	Ives	64.8%
1950	Lynch	31.1%	Dewey	68.9%
1946	Mead	23.3%	Dewey	76.6%
1942	Bennett	27.9%	Dewey	72.1%
1938	Lehman	34.9%	Dewey	65.1%
1936	Lehman	40.0%	Bleakley	60.0%
1934	Lehman	50.4%	Moses	49.6%
1932	Lehman	48.4%	Donovan	51.6%
1930	Roosevelt	49.9%	Tuttle	50.1%
1928	Roosevelt	44.1%	Ottinger	55.9%
1926	Smith	44.9%	Mills	55.1%
1924	Smith	41.0%	T. Roosevelt	59.0%

Source: New York State Board of Elections and the New York Red Book.
*Proportions compiled from vote for two major party candidates by MIPO.

At the presidential level, vote tallies in the suburbs reveal continued Republican dominance. In the past sixty years, only one Democratic presidential candidate outpolled his Republican opponent. President Johnson received 59.9% of the vote in 1964 (See Table 3.8).

Table 3.8
New York Suburban Vote for President 1924-1984

	Democratic Candidate		Republican Candidate		Other Candidates
1984	Mondale	37.5%	Reagan	62.3%	0.2%
1980	Carter	34.5%	Reagan	55.9%	9.6%
1976	Carter	46.5%	Ford	53.1%	0.5%
1972	McGovern	34.6%	Nixon	65.1%	0.2%
1968	Humphrey	40.8%	Nixon	52.6%	6.7%
1964	Johnson	59.9%	Goldwater	40.0%	0.1%
1960	Kennedy	43.4%	Nixon	56.4%	0.1%
1956	Stevenson	28.2%	Eisenhower	71.7%	——
1952	Stevenson	30.1%	Eisenhower	69.5%	0.4%
1948	Truman	30.1%	Dewey	66.1%	3.8%
1944	Roosevelt	35.4%	Dewey	64.3%	0.3%
1940	Roosevelt	36.1%	Wilkie	63.7%	0.2%
1936	Roosevelt	44.8%	Landon	53.2%	2.0%
1932	Roosevelt	44.6%	Hoover	52.8%	2.7%
1928	Smith	37.8%	Hoover	59.8%	2.5%
1924	Davis	23.2%	Coolidge	66.2%	10.6%

Source: New York State Board of Elections and the New York Red Book. Suburban vote compiled by MIPO.

The evidence points to many noteworthy changes in the relationships which have existed between political leaders and this electorate. Despite continued Republican successes for many offices, there have been shifts in the affiliations and voting choices of the suburban electorate. It is interesting to note that these changes began before Watergate. Rather than becoming an even stronger GOP bloc, today's suburban electorate is far different from what existed prior to the population boom. A new electorate has emerged in the region.

Although this changed electoral arena may have created the possibility of a successful political appeal by a Democratic figure like Mario Cuomo, it by no means accounts for the degree of success he has enjoyed, nor does it explain the basis of his appeal. An analysis of the relationship which exists between Mario Cuomo and the suburban electorate requires examination into the current political attitudes of that electorate—its ideological focus, its opinions on issues of public policy, and its perception of Mario Cuomo.

Contemporary suburbanites differ from the conventional wisdom which has characterized them as ideological conservatives, advocates of less government intervention, and single-issue voters. Instead, this electorate possesses a moderate ideological framework, is not opposed to government intervention into domestic policy, and has broadly based issue concerns.

In terms of the political ideology of present-day suburban voters, the dominant self-image is middle-of-the-road. 48.8% of suburban voters see themselves as "moderate" politically, whereas 19.2% see themselves as "liberal," and 32.0% view themselves as "conservative." This change in ideological orientation has resulted from gradual developments in the suburbs. First, the increase in Democratic and Independent identification has been an important component in shaping the ideological complexion of the region. More than half of the Democrats and the Independents consider themselves to be "moderate." Coupled with the 31.0% of the Democrats and 18.0% of the Independents who see themselves as "liberal," the change in partisanship in the suburbs has had a major influence on moderating the formerly conservative political orientation of the region (See Table 3.9). In addition, the large number of professionally employed workers contributes to the "moderate" stance in the four counties. As a group, professional workers are more middle-of-the-road politically (See Table 3.9).

Table 3.9
New York Suburban Respondent's Party Identification and
Occupation By Respondent's Ideology

	Liberal	Moderate	Conservative
Party Identification			
Democrat	31.0%	51.7%	17.3%
Republican	12.6%	44.5%	42.9%
Independent	18.0%	52.2%	29.8%
Occupation			
Manual	27.2%	36.3%	36.5%
Clerical/Sales	21.6%	44.9%	33.5%
Managerial	15.5%	46.6%	37.9%
Professional	18.9%	59.8%	21.4%

When this electorate is classified by its ideology and party identification, the region's diversity becomes apparent. Liberal and moderate-Democrats and liberal and moderate-Independents comprise over half of today's suburban vote. Although migrants from New York City comprise a larger part of this group, due to their greater Democratic identification, both former New York City residents and suburban residents who have never lived in the city are contributing to the present ideological and party variation in the region, comprising 56.0% and 44.3% of this group, respectively (See Table 3.10).

The region's electorate has strayed from its conservative, homogeneous image, contributing to a broadened issue focus. In terms of public policy issues, early migrants to the suburbs left behind a highly organized urban community to arrive in a loosely integrated suburban setting. A new issue agenda had to be developed. Although the concerns of the newcomers initially matched their reasons for moving to the suburbs and

Table 3.10

New York Suburban Respondent's Combined Ideological and
Party Identification

	Total NY Suburbs	Resided in New York City	Never Resided in New York City
Liberal-Democrat	8.1%	9.7%	6.5%
Moderate-Democrat	13.5%	17.2%	9.8%
Conservative-Democrat	4.5%	5.0%	4.1%
Liberal-Republican	4.2%	2.7%	5.6%
Moderate-Republican	14.7%	12.3%	17.0%
Conservative-Republican	14.2%	12.8%	15.7%
Liberal-Independent	7.4%	7.6%	7.1%
Moderate-Independent	21.3%	21.5%	20.9%
Conservative-Independent	12.2%	10.9%	13.2%

centered around local taxes, property values, and crime, current concerns of the suburban electorate reflect its diversity and urbanized character. Suburban voters have a more broadened focus which includes issues such as senior citizen care, the environment, day care, job training, and discrimination against minorities and others. Survey data substantiate this point. Today's suburban voters express a wide range of concerns about what they consider to be the number one problem facing the state. Although taxes, property values, and crime still occupy a major place in the voters' outlook, they are joined in importance by such different issues as employment opportunities, human service needs, housing, the environment, and roads and mass transportation. In addition, there is currently little difference between the issue concerns expressed by those suburbanites who left New York City and other suburban residents (See Table 3.11).

Table 3.11

New York Suburban Respondent's View of the Most Important Problem
Facing New York State

"What do you consider to be the number one problem facing New York State?"

	Total NY Suburbs	Resided in New York City	Never Resided in New York City
Taxes	21.1%	20.8%	21.4%
Jobs	16.6%	18.0%	15.2%
Other Economic Issues	6.5%	6.8%	6.2%
Human Services	13.7%	12.7%	14.8%
Poverty			
Elderly			
Education			
Other			
Environment	10.0%	9.7%	10.1%
Crime	9.1%	12.0%	6.3%
Housing	8.7%	7.9%	9.6%
Roads and Mass			
Transportation	3.9%	3.7%	4.1%
Other Social Issues	3.4%	2.9%	3.9%
Abortion			
Moral Decline			
Other	6.9%	5.6%	8.4%

Given the ideological character and issue focus of present-day suburbanites, it is not surprising that voters' preferences on various policy choices differ dramatically from earlier views. For example, suburban voters express positive feelings toward government intervention into domestic policy. By a ratio of 3:1, voters believe that government should be involved in programs for housing, health care, and jobs. The idea that an individual should "work things out on his own," a laissez-faire approach, is less popular (See Table 3.12). Similarly, by a ratio of 3:2 suburban voters believe that the income gap separating the rich and the poor in this country should be reduced by the government becoming involved in addressing the inequity. Underlying this belief is the perception that current

economic policies do not benefit all segments of society. Voters
in the four county region believe by a ratio of 2:1 that not everyone
is sharing in the economic recovery. The suburban electorate also
supports greater government involvement in improving the environment. By a ratio of 6:1, these voters advocate a more active
government role. Voters also indicate their willingness to support a political leader who advocates increased federal spending
to cities and greater federal commitment to mass transportation
(See Table 3.12).

Table 3.12

New York Suburban Respondent's Views on the Role of
Government and Candidate Positions

"Using the numbers 1 to 5, with 1 meaning strongly agree and 5 meaning strongly disagree, please tell me how you feel about each of the following statements."

	Agree (1 & 2)	Neutral (3)	Disagree (4 & 5)
"Government should not get involved in programs for housing, health care, and jobs and should let each person work things out on his own."	22.3%	15.4%	62.3%
"Government should concern itself with narrowing the income differences between the rich and the poor in this country."	52.7%	16.8%	30.5%
"Everyone is sharing in the economic recovery."	24.1%	32.2%	43.7%
"Government should spend more time improving and protecting the environment."	71.9%	15.4%	12.7%

"Would you be more likely or less likely to vote for a candidate who does each of the
following? If it makes no difference to you, please say so."

	More Likely	No Difference	Less Likely
"A candidate who wants to increase federal aid to cities."	62.2%	24.9%	12.8%
"A candidate who wants to increase spending for mass transportation."	61.3%	28.6%	10.1%

Concerning government job training for the unemployed and government spending for the poor and the elderly, the data suggest that these voters have a favorable view towards such government sponsored programs (See Table 3.13). Particularly revealing about these attitudes on government's role is that they remain largely intact even following the introduction of fiscal matters. Suburban voters overwhelmingly reject the notion of supporting a candidate who would balance the budget by cutting social program spending. In addition, despite its concern over high taxes, the electorate exhibits a liberal policy outlook by opposing a tax cut if this resulted in a reduction in government services (See Table 3.13).

Table 3.13

New York Suburban Respondent's Views on Candidate Positions

"Would you be more likely or less likely to vote for a candidate who does each of the following? If it makes no difference to you, please say so."

	More Likely	No Difference	Less Likely
"A candidate who advocates increased spending for job training for the unemployed."	74.9%	11.4%	13.7%
"A candidate who advocates increasing government programs for the poor and the elderly."	76.6%	10.0%	13.4%
"A candidate who wants to balance the budget by cutting social programs."	22.7%	6.8%	70.6%
"A candidate who wants to cut taxes by cutting government services."	27.7%	8.4%	64.0%

Not only do suburban voters favor government's continued role in domestic policy, they desire a redirection in priorities away from defense toward spending for social programs. In relating their policy preferences in defense and social spending to the national budget, this electorate believes that less money should be spent on national defense and that more money should be allocated for social programs (See Table 3.14).

This analysis is facilitated by looking at the party affiliation and ideology of the suburban electorate. A majority of liberal-Democrats, moderate-Democrats, liberal-Independents, and moderate-Independents favors a reduction in defense spending. The remaining groups typically prefer that defense spending be maintained at current levels. Regarding social program spending, a majority of the same constituency, liberal-Democrats, moderate-Democrats, liberal-Independents, and moderate-Independents, prefers increases in spending for social programs. Pluralities of the remaining groups either favor that spending be increased or maintained at current levels. In no case is a majority of any group in favor of an increase in defense spending or a reduction in social program spending (See Table 3.14). In examining the suburban electorate's views on cutbacks in federal social programs, this same group of voters, joined by a majority of liberal-Republicans, opposes further social program reductions (See Table 3.14).

Table 3.14

New York Suburban Respondent's Views on the National Budget by Ideology and Party Identification

Spending for National Defense

"Regarding the national budget, do you think we should spend more money for national defense, less money for national defense, or current spending is about right?"

	More Money	About Right	Less Money
New York Suburbs	13.2%	40.6%	46.2%
Liberal-Democrat	9.8%	22.3%	67.9%
Moderate-Democrat	7.5%	27.2%	65.4%
Conservative-Democrat	15.3%	37.8%	46.8%
Liberal-Republican	18.7%	55.2%	26.1%
Moderate-Republican	11.9%	50.0%	38.1%

Table 3.14 Continued

	More Money	About Right	Less Money
Conservative-Republican	20.1%	57.3%	22.5%
Liberal-Independent	18.6%	29.4%	52.0%
Moderate-Independent	8.5%	37.6%	53.9%
Conservative-Independent	12.0%	52.6%	35.4%

Spending for Social Programs

"Regarding the national budget, do you think we should spend more money for social programs, less money for social programs, or current spending is about right?"

	More Money	About Right	Less Money
New York Suburbs	50.5%	34.1%	15.5%
Liberal-Democrat	71.2%	20.0%	8.8%
Moderate-Democrat	55.1%	37.2%	7.7%
Conservative-Democrat	48.6%	36.8%	14.6%
Liberal-Republican	41.6%	43.4%	15.0%
Moderate-Republican	43.7%	43.6%	12.7%
Conservative-Republican	34.9%	40.5%	24.6%
Liberal-Independent	77.0%	18.2%	4.8%
Moderate-Independent	52.4%	30.2%	17.5%
Conservative-Independent	35.1%	41.1%	23.8%

Cutbacks in Social Program Spending

"Do you feel that federal cutbacks in social programs have been too much, not enough, or about right?"

	Too Much	About Right	Not Enough
New York Suburbs	48.0%	33.8%	18.2%
Liberal-Democrat	79.9%	14.7%	5.3%
Moderate-Democrat	70.5%	18.2%	11.3%
Conservative-Democrat	26.6%	43.3%	30.2%
Liberal-Republican	53.7%	26.3%	20.0%
Moderate-Republican	41.7%	42.3%	16.0%
Conservative-Republican	23.2%	42.4%	34.4%
Liberal-Independent	63.0%	26.4%	10.6%
Moderate-Independent	50.7%	32.3%	17.0%
Conservative-Independent	27.4%	50.4%	22.3%

Public sentiment in favor of social programs is also illustrated by suburban support for increases in state spending to offset any further reductions in federal spending. 60.9% of suburban voters prefer that New York State increase spending for social programs to make up for any further federal cutbacks. 29.2% do not support an increase in state spending.[9] These attitudes are prevalent both among suburban voters who migrated from New York City and suburbanites who never resided in the city. There is little difference between New York City migrants and other suburban residents on these issues (See Table 3.15).

Table 3.15
Former New York City Residents vs. Non-New York City Residents in the New York Suburbs on Issues and Candidates

"Using the numbers 1 to 5, with 1 meaning strongly agree and 5 meaning strongly disagree, please tell me how you feel about each of the following statements."

		Agree (1 & 2)	Neutral (3)	Disagree (4 & 5)
"Government should not get involved in programs for housing, health care, and jobs and should let each person work things out on his own."	Total NY Suburbs	22.3%	15.4%	62.3%
	Resided in NYC	21.8%	16.2%	62.0%
	Never Resided NYC	22.3%	14.7%	62.9%
"Government should concern itself with narrowing the income differences between the rich and the poor in this country."	Total NY Suburbs	52.7%	16.8%	30.5%
	Resided in NYC	50.7%	18.0%	31.4%
	Never Resided NYC	54.9%	15.6%	29.6%
"Everyone is sharing in the economic recovery."	Total NY Suburbs	24.1%	32.2%	43.7%
	Resided in NYC	24.8%	31.7%	43.5%
	Never Resided NYC	23.3%	32.7%	44.1%
"Government should spend more time improving and protecting the environment."	Total NY Suburbs	71.9%	15.4%	12.7%
	Resided in NYC	70.9%	14.6%	14.6%
	Never Resided NYC	72.6%	16.4%	11.0%

"Would you be more likely or less likely to vote for a candidate who does each of the following? If it makes no difference to you, please say so."

		More Likely	No Difference	Less Likely
"A candidate who wants to increase federal aid to cities."	Total NY Suburbs	62.2%	24.9%	12.8%
	Resided in NYC	67.9%	24.8%	7.3%
	Never Resided NYC	56.1%	25.7%	18.1%

Table 3.15 Continued

		More Likely	No Difference	Less Likely
"A candidate who wants to increase spending for mass transportation."	Total NY Suburbs	61.3%	28.6%	10.1%
	Resided in NYC	63.4%	23.7%	12.9%
	Never Resided NYC	58.5%	33.5%	8.0%
"A candidate who advocates increased spending for job training for the unemployed."	Total NY Suburbs	74.9%	11.4%	13.7%
	Resided in NYC	75.7%	8.7%	15.7%
	Never Resided NYC	74.3%	13.9%	11.8%
"A candidate who advocates increasing government programs for the poor and the elderly."	Total NY Suburbs	76.6%	10.0%	13.4%
	Resided in NYC	75.5%	8.8%	15.7%
	Never Resided NYC	78.0%	10.8%	11.2%
"A candidate who wants to balance the budget by cutting social programs."	Total NY Suburbs	22.7%	6.8%	70.6%
	Resided in NYC	23.4%	6.6%	70.0%
	Never Resided NYC	22.1%	6.7%	71.2%
"A candidate who wants to cut taxes by cutting government services."	Total NY Suburbs	27.7%	8.4%	64.0%
	Resided in NYC	23.4%	9.0%	67.6%
	Never Resided NYC	32.3%	7.4%	60.4%

		More Money	About Right	Less Money
"Regarding the national budget, do you think we should spend more money for national defense, less money for national defense, or current spending is about right?"	Total NY Suburbs	13.2%	40.6%	46.2%
	Resided in NYC	12.4%	40.1%	47.5%
	Never Resided NYC	13.9%	41.1%	45.0%
"Regarding the national budget, do you think we should spend more money for social programs, less money for social programs, or current spending is about right?"	Total NY Suburbs	50.5%	34.1%	15.5%
	Resided in NYC	50.9%	33.7%	15.5%
	Never Resided NYC	50.4%	34.3%	15.3%

		Too Much	About Right	Not Enough
"Do you feel that federal cutbacks in social programs have been too much, not enough, or about right?"	Total NY Suburbs	48.0%	33.8%	18.2%
	Resided in NYC	49.2%	33.8%	17.0%
	Never Resided NYC	47.1%	33.6%	19.3%

THE CUOMO FACTOR

This discussion has examined the contemporary political fabric of suburbia. The suburbs surrounding New York City were gradually transformed following World War II as new people settled in the area and the region grew. As a result, the political character of the suburbs is far different from what existed several decades ago. There has been an erosion of partisanship, but heightened voter interest in politics and issues. Contrary to the traditional perception, these voters possess a broadly based issue focus, advocate an active role for government in domestic policy, and support a continued commitment to social program spending.

Chapter Four

The New York Suburban Electorate and Mario Cuomo

Mario Cuomo's extensive political appeal in the New York suburbs results from the region's present makeup and his sensitivity to the importance of the region's voters. This chapter explores the relationship between the suburban electorate and Mario Cuomo by examining Cuomo's suburban political appeal, how he has gained the support of these voters, and this electorate's perception of him.

Although Governor Cuomo's political appeal among suburban voters is now wide-spread, his popularity developed gradually. Prior to the 1982 Democratic gubernatorial primary, suburban voters were very familiar with Mayor Koch in contrast to the then relatively unknown Lieutenant Governor Cuomo. Cuomo did well in the region, but his popularity was not outstanding. As noted in *The New York Times,* "The Cuomo victory pattern was to lose the city just barely along with its suburbs...and to swamp Mr. Koch upstate...."[1] However, even the vote Cuomo received in the suburbs can be partially attributed to Koch's damaging interview with *Playboy* magazine rather than to positive feelings of suburbanites for Cuomo. In the interview, Koch spoke disparagingly about the banality of life outside the city.

In the 1982 general election against Lew Lehrman, Cuomo's showing among suburban voters was somewhat stronger. Cuomo carried two of the four suburban counties, and his vote in the

67

region compared favorably with his statewide total. Cuomo also fared better in the suburbs than upstate (See Table 4.1). Overall, Cuomo fashioned this statewide victory by receiving close to the usual Democratic majorities in the city and running nearly even with Lehrman in the suburbs (See Table 4.1).[2] Additionally, exit polls revealed some unusual patterns in this general election. Among high income groups, the ABC News exit poll showed significant inroads for a Democratic candidate. In those households whose combined family income before taxes exceeded $40,000, Cuomo received 55% of the vote to Lehrman's 44%. Also, among salaried wage earners, Cuomo received 56% of the vote to Lehrman's 42%. Both of these percentages exceeded his statewide tally. In addition, the CBS News/*New York Times* exit poll of New York State voters showed Cuomo trailing Lehrman by just 1% among professional/managerial workers. Although these two exit polls employed different methods, the data indicated support for Cuomo at the time among voters who comprise a substantial part of the suburban electorate. As in the Democratic primary, Cuomo's suburban vote in the general election was bolstered by factors independent of his own efforts. His vote was affected by Republican Party organization squabbles in Nassau County and the presence of Westchester County Executive Al DelBello as his running mate.

Table 4.1
New York State 1982 Gubernatorial Election

	Cuomo	Lehrman	Other Candidates
New York State	50.9%	47.5%	1.6%
Region			
Upstate	42.0%	56.7%	1.3%
New York City	67.1%	31.3%	1.6%
Suburbs	47.1%	50.7%	2.2%

Table 4.1 Continued

	Cuomo	Lehrman	Other Candidates
Suburban Counties			
Nassau	46.8%	50.7%	2.5%
Rockland	49.5%	48.8%	1.6%
Suffolk	44.4%	53.4%	2.2%
Westchester	50.2%	48.1%	1.7%

Source: New York State Board of Elections. Regional breakdown compiled by MIPO.

In the first MIPO survey on the Cuomo Administration conducted six months after he assumed office, Cuomo's suburban political appeal was apparent. Cuomo's statewide popularity at the time was 57.0% while his support in the suburbs was 63.9%. Following Cuomo's keynote address at the Democratic National Convention in the summer of 1984, both his statewide and suburban popularity soared (See Table 4.2). This address provided Cuomo with the opportunity to define his approach to government, and he utilized the forum to communicate his themes effectively. Cuomo's "excellent" rating in the suburbs, for example, went from 6.9% in June 1984, to 23.5% in September 1984.

Table 4.2
Governor Cuomo's Performance Rating

"Would you rate the job Governor Mario Cuomo is doing in office as excellent, good, fair, or poor?"

New York State	Excellent	Good	Fair	Poor
June 1986	19.4%	51.2%	23.4%	5.9%
January 1986	15.7%	52.7%	25.0%	6.6%
October 1985	16.0%	52.1%	25.4%	6.6%
June 1985	18.4%	51.2%	22.3%	8.1%
January 1985	15.1%	49.3%	26.5%	9.1%
September 1984	21.9%	44.2%	25.9%	8.0%
June 1984	8.3%	50.7%	32.3%	8.6%

Table 4.2 Continued

	Excellent	Good	Fair	Poor
January 1984	11.6%	49.0%	31.5%	8.0%
September 1983	9.3%	47.2%	35.5%	8.0%
June 1983	11.6%	45.4%	34.1%	8.8%

Region	Excellent	Good	Fair	Poor
Upstate				
June 1986	16.0%	52.9%	25.2%	5.9%
January 1986	15.8%	47.9%	27.9%	8.4%
October 1985	12.9%	50.2%	28.3%	8.6%
June 1985	13.9%	50.1%	26.2%	9.8%
January 1985	12.3%	47.8%	27.9%	12.1%
September 1984	18.6%	40.4%	30.2%	10.9%
June 1984	6.1%	47.9%	33.1%	12.8%
January 1984	8.7%	47.5%	32.2%	11.5%
September 1983	8.8%	40.5%	39.6%	11.2%
June 1983	9.1%	42.6%	34.8%	13.5%
New York City				
June 1986	23.0%	49.3%	20.9%	6.8%
January 1986	14.9%	59.4%	19.7%	6.1%
October 1985	21.5%	51.6%	22.9%	3.9%
June 1985	20.6%	52.4%	21.8%	5.2%
January 1985	16.1%	49.0%	28.2%	6.7%
September 1984	24.7%	42.1%	27.7%	5.5%
June 1984	12.3%	52.3%	29.8%	5.6%
January 1984	14.5%	50.4%	29.4%	5.7%
September 1983	12.2%	56.0%	28.2%	3.6%
June 1983	14.3%	44.9%	36.1%	4.7%
Suburbs				
June 1986	20.5%	51.1%	23.9%	4.5%
January 1986	16.6%	52.1%	27.1%	4.2%
October 1985	19.3%	52.7%	23.5%	4.5%
June 1985	23.4%	51.8%	15.6%	9.3%
January 1985	18.8%	52.7%	21.5%	7.0%
September 1984	23.5%	53.9%	15.9%	6.8%
June 1984	6.9%	54.0%	34.4%	4.8%
January 1984	13.2%	49.9%	32.7%	4.2%
September 1983	6.4%	48.0%	37.5%	8.0%
June 1983	12.4%	51.5%	29.4%	6.6%

Cuomo's overall job performance rating has remained high ever since, and his suburban score has been exceptionally strong.

The New York Suburban Electorate and Mario Cuomo

An examination of Cuomo's suburban popularity reveals that his approval rating has been high in each of the four counties where he has consistently received between 70% and 75% (See Table 4.3). In addition, his rating in the suburbs has often exceeded his New York City response. In carrying New York State by a landslide in 1986, Cuomo defeated O'Rourke in each of the four suburban counties by wide margins. In this contest, Cuomo negated an effort by the Republicans to reclaim the suburban region. Not only were most of the Republican statewide candidates from the area, but the O'Rourke campaign emphasized the importance of the suburbs. In spelling out his strategy, O'Rourke noted, "We've got to carry Westchester, which Lehrman didn't do...and we have to carry Long Island."[3]

Cuomo's popularity is further understood by examining various population characteristics in the region. For example, the political party and ideology of these voters reveal the nature of Cuomo's suburban constituency. Cuomo attracts overwhelming support from Democrats, and he has the approval of more than two-thirds of the Independents, and nearly two-thirds of the Republicans. Cuomo also has substantial appeal across the electorate ideologically. However, voters who see themselves as left-of-center and middle-of-the-road are more likely to approve of Cuomo than are those who see themselves as right-of-center (See Table 4.3).

Governor Cuomo attracts overwhelming support from seven of the nine subgroups within the electorate created by combining these party and ideology categories. Cuomo receives high marks across party lines from voters who see themselves as liberal or moderate ideologically. He is particularly strong, not surprisingly, among liberal-Democrats and moderate-Democrats. He is also favorably viewed by large numbers of Independents and Republicans. Although Cuomo does receive the approval of a majority of conservative-Republicans and conservative-

Independents, his support among these conservative voters is generally weaker. The exception to this pattern is among conservative-Democrats, who rate him highly (See Table 4.3).

Cuomo's strength among suburban voters is also revealed by reviewing the education, occupation, and income of the electorate. Cuomo's appeal is strongest among those suburban voters with high levels of education, and he fares well among those who are employed in professional occupations. Income variations in the population do not exhibit a consistent pattern. Cuomo is very popular among all income groups (See Table 4.3). In addition, Mario Cuomo's performance rating is only slightly higher among suburban voters who once lived in New York City than it is among other suburban residents. He receives a 75.0% approval rating from New York City migrants and a 68.9% approval rating from those suburbanites who never resided in the city.

Table 4.3
Governor Cuomo's Performance Rating in the New York Suburbs

	Excellent	Good	Fair	Poor
October 1985	19.3%	52.7%	23.5%	4.5%
County				
Nassau	20.3%	53.8%	22.5%	3.5%
Rockland	20.7%	50.9%	24.3%	4.1%
Suffolk	20.1%	50.9%	23.7%	5.3%
Westchester	16.2%	54.3%	24.3%	5.3%
Party Identification				
Democrat	27.1%	54.5%	15.7%	2.7%
Republican	13.2%	51.5%	29.0%	6.3%
Independent	20.2%	51.5%	24.1%	4.2%
Ideology				
Liberal	27.4%	53.6%	17.4%	1.7%
Moderate	21.5%	53.7%	21.5%	3.3%
Conservative	11.5%	47.8%	31.9%	8.7%

Table 4.3 Continued

	Excellent	Good	Fair	Poor
Combined Ideological and Party Identification				
Liberal-Democrat	35.3%	53.1%	11.6%	0.0%
Moderate-Democrat	27.0%	53.9%	16.0%	3.1%
Conservative-Democrat	16.8%	57.2%	19.0%	7.1%
Liberal-Republican	10.3%	62.1%	25.1%	2.5%
Moderate-Republican	14.9%	53.8%	26.6%	4.7%
Conservative-Republican	11.1%	45.0%	34.6%	9.3%
Liberal-Independent	28.8%	49.5%	18.5%	3.2%
Moderate-Independent	22.2%	54.8%	21.4%	1.6%
Conservative-Independent	10.2%	44.8%	35.0%	10.0%
Education				
Less than High School	12.7%	41.3%	37.0%	9.0%
High School	16.1%	52.9%	24.2%	6.8%
Some College	16.9%	54.8%	23.2%	5.1%
College	20.0%	55.8%	22.3%	1.9%
Grad/Professional	28.1%	50.5%	19.7%	1.7%
Occupation				
Manual	11.4%	57.8%	26.8%	4.1%
Clerical/Sales	17.9%	51.4%	23.9%	6.8%
Managerial	18.9%	50.7%	24.5%	5.8%
Professional	22.0%	55.1%	20.9%	2.1%
Income				
Under $10,000	26.5%	34.4%	33.4%	5.7%
$10,000-$24,000	15.7%	58.8%	19.8%	5.7%
$25,000-$40,000	19.4%	52.6%	23.4%	4.7%
$41,000-$60,000	18.3%	49.6%	26.1%	6.0%
Over $60,000	24.2%	52.6%	20.4%	2.8%

In terms of Cuomo's image as governor, voters throughout the region give him high marks. Overwhelming numbers of voters believe that he is a good leader for New York State and takes clearly defined positions on issues. Voters also approve, but to a lesser degree, of Cuomo's playing an active role in national politics. They do not believe that his national activities limit the attention he gives to New York State (See Table 4.4). Cuomo's ability to relate national issues to the state's electorate has come across consistently.

Table 4.4

New York Suburban Respondent's Assessments of Governor Mario Cuomo

"I'm going to read you several statements about Governor Mario Cuomo. Please tell me if you agree or disagree with each one."

	Agree	Disagree	No Opinion
"Governor Cuomo is a good leader for New York State."	80.6%	15.3%	4.1%
"Governor Cuomo takes clearly defined positions on issues."	69.8%	22.0%	8.3%
"Governor Cuomo is paying too much attention to national politics and not enough attention to New York State."	31.6%	58.2%	10.2%

For the most part, Cuomo is favorably assessed throughout the suburban electorate. Democrats, Republicans, and Independents, liberals, moderates, and conservatives, all rate Cuomo strongly on his leadership abilities and on taking clearly defined positions on issues. On the question of Cuomo's role in national affairs, voters tend to split along partisan and ideological lines. Voters who identify with the Republican Party and who see themselves as right-of-center ideologically are more likely to view Cuomo's performance unfavorably (See Table 4.5). On the whole, the data suggest that Governor Cuomo's popularity among suburban voters, although initially limited, is now widespread.

Cuomo's political appeal with suburban voters also reflects electoral trends which have been occurring nationwide. Recent

Table 4.5

New York Suburban Respondent's Assessments of Governor Mario Cuomo and the Respondent's Ideology and Party Identification

"I'm going to read you several statements about Governor Mario Cuomo. Please tell me if you agree or disagree with each one."

"Governor Cuomo is a good leader for New York State."

	Agree	Disagree	No Opinion
Ideology			
Liberal	88.7%	7.6%	3.7%
Moderate	84.0%	13.2%	2.8%
Conservative	69.5%	24.2%	6.3%
Party Identification			
Democrat	88.8%	8.3%	2.9%
Republican	74.4%	18.7%	7.0%
Independent	81.3%	16.8%	1.9%

"Governor Cuomo takes clearly defined positions on issues."

	Agree	Disagree	No Opinion
Ideology			
Liberal	77.0%	15.2%	7.9%
Moderate	70.1%	21.6%	8.3%
Conservative	63.8%	28.2%	8.0%
Party Identification			
Democrat	78.6%	13.4%	8.0%
Republican	65.8%	26.5%	7.7%
Independent	67.4%	23.7%	8.9%

"Governor Cuomo is paying too much attention to national politics and not enough attention to New York State."

	Agree	Disagree	No Opinion
Ideology			
Liberal	26.1%	65.7%	8.2%
Moderate	27.9%	63.9%	8.3%
Conservative	43.5%	44.7%	11.9%
Party Identification			
Democrat	21.1%	71.5%	7.3%
Republican	37.6%	49.0%	13.4%
Independent	33.3%	57.2%	9.5%

elections have led several political analysts to suggest that a shift is occurring in the support for the two major political parties. They point to changes in the American economic system since World War II which have resulted in a greater proportion of the workforce now involved in research and development, communications, education, and advanced technology. This relatively new group of voters tends to be supportive of government social and environmental programs. According to Alan Gitelson, "Scholars view this as a new coalition that unites in the Democratic Party the less advantaged who benefit from the government's social assistance programs and the affluent technological class who are concerned with the quality of life for themselves and others."[4]

While the Republican Party has made inroads into the traditional Democratic coalition, particularly among working-class voters and in the South, the Democratic Party has the potential for broadening its appeal to include many categories of voters usually reserved for the GOP: higher income families, the better educated, and residents of middle-size cities and suburbs.[5] As William Crotty pointed out, "a coalition that was built upon a working-class base has expanded and increased its appeal to middle and upper-class professionals."[6] Democratic Party gains among these socioeconomic groups suggest that many Democrats who made the transition from working class to middle class and professional occupations during the postwar boom retained their partisan loyalties, as well as an ongoing belief in a liberal policy agenda.[7] Ladd has noted that because this large group of professional/managerial individuals are detached from traditional business concerns, they are supportive of more liberal positions.[8]

While the national shift in voter sentiment is real, its magnitude is easily overstated. Even during the New Deal, when blue-collar workers provided Roosevelt with whopping majorities, his appeal to other segments of the electorate was also strong. In the New Deal period, middle-class voters moved into the Democratic fold as the Democrats challenged the Republicans for their failure to produce prosperity. One national survey at the time indicated that 18% of the middle-class voters who supported Hoover in 1928, switched to Roosevelt in 1932. A Gallup Poll revealed that businessmen split evenly in 1932 and professionals gave Roosevelt a 53% − 47% edge.[9] Although definitions of the New Deal coalition have typically excluded these upscale voters, their support was prevalent.

More recently, despite GOP landslides at the presidential level, support for the Democratic Party remains among these higher socioeconomic segments of the electorate, and the potential for expansion is apparent. For example, although the GOP share of the national vote in 1956 and 1984 was virtually the same, 58% and 59%, respectively, there was a shift in the coalitional support for the parties. In 1984, as compared to 1956, the GOP performed 14% better in the South than its national average, whereas the GOP share fell by 8% among college educated voters and 10% among white-collar voters.[10]

Mario Cuomo's success in appealing to highly educated, professional workers, and to others in the New York suburbs is in keeping with this trend. The establishment of such a relationship, however, is by no means automatic. The attractiveness of a political leader to these voters must be firmly grounded. The political leader must understand voters' concerns and seek their support.

Mario Cuomo is in touch with this potential source of growing political support for the Democratic Party and understands the necessity in New York State politics of attracting these suburban voters. He commented, "If you mean by the Democratic coalition that we have to piece together special interest groups—ethnics, blacks, labor unions—that's not the best way to build a party...You have to pick up affluent people who I refer to as the enlightened affluents...What you have to do is convince people of the nation that [they] can afford to be compassionate...."[11]

In attempting to expand his political appeal in New York State politics, Mario Cuomo has effectively addressed this key concern for Democrats. As pollster Mark Penn observed, "The Democratic Party has a serious problem in the suburbs that it is going to have to deal with...The core Democratic constituencies haven't really defected...The question for the Democrats is not what to do in New York City, but how to reach out to the suburbs...so that they can have a chance of winning New York State elections."[12]

These suburbs represented, from Cuomo's perspective, an electoral necessity in 1982 and a return ticket to Albany in 1986. According to former Cuomo adviser Tim Russert, "Anyone who is sophisticated politically recognizes the importance of the suburbs...We knew the importance of the suburbs. You really do focus on that. If you want to stay in office, it is a necessity."[13] Cuomo has been especially effective in establishing a political appeal in the region. As one observer of New York politics commented, Cuomo, in attempting to broaden his political base, "has solved the puzzle of a Democrat in the suburbs because, more than any other contemporary political figure, he understands how the pieces fit together."

In assessing the 1986 election results, the suburbs assumed a special role. Cuomo's expanded political appeal in the suburbs allowed him to pursue a record-setting strategy. As Cuomo's Director of Communications, Gary Fryer, noted, "When you examine the possibility of winning by a large majority, [the suburbs] are essential. We have enjoyed for better than three years some abnormally high numbers in these areas...that provides for us an enormous base upon which to build a candidacy. It allows us to pay more attention to upstate while basically trying to maintain the popularity we have in those areas as opposed to trying to create it. So, in that respect they become key to a large victory, but they are always important to any victory."[14]

Although Cuomo and his staff do not calculate how each of their decisions will be received by the suburban electorate, there is a sensitivity on their part to the importance of the region and the impact of Cuomo's positions on its voters. A Cuomo adviser commented, "The 'Rebuild New York' bond issue is a very good example...We knew that the suburbs were crucial in order to pass the bond issue, and we spent an inordinate amount of time with the Long Island delegation to the state legislature...The support of Long Island was extremely crucial in passing it statewide. That was a very important calculation...We looked at the previous bond issues and knew that upstaters were by and large opposed to bond issues, the city would be supportive...and that the suburbs would be marginal. You target your marginal vote." Other issues that Cuomo has stressed during his term in office have enjoyed wide popularity within the suburbs. His handling of several regional issues such as the use of the Shoreham Nuclear Power Plant, the failure of the Long Island Lighting Company (LILCO) to respond to Hurricane Gloria, the passage of the mandatory seatbelt law, and the adoption of an increase in the state's alcohol purchase age from 19 to 21 have all been important to Cuomo's relationship with suburban voters (See Table 4.6). His recent effort to make LILCO a public utility has been particularly effective. As political analyst Alan Chartock commented, "Cuomo's campaign against LILCO has been so devastating that even the Republicans who have traditionally protected the utilities have had to turn tail and run for cover."[15]

In addition, although New York voters had supported Ronald Reagan in both 1980 and 1984, there was the belief that

---

Table 4.6

New York State Regional Breakdown of Selected Issues

The Vote for New York State's 1983 Transportation Bond Issue*

	Yes	No
New York State	53.1%	46.9%
Region		
Upstate	43.6%	56.4%
New York City	71.7%	28.3%
Suburbs	57.8%	42.2%

"Do you favor or oppose the new seatbelt law in New York State?"

	Favor	Oppose	Unsure
January 1985	57.9%	38.3%	3.8%
Region			
Upstate	43.4%	51.3%	5.2%
New York City	75.0%	23.1%	1.9%
Suburbs	60.1%	35.8%	4.1%

"Do you favor or oppose a proposal in New York State to raise the drinking age from 19 to 21?"

	Favor	Oppose	Unsure
January 1985	70.7%	25.7%	3.6%
Region			
Upstate	62.0%	33.3%	4.7%
New York City	73.5%	22.8%	3.7%
Suburbs	82.8%	15.7%	1.5%

*Source: New York State Board of Elections. Regional breakdown compiled by MIPO.

Cuomo's opposition to Reagan on specific issues would not damage him politically either statewide or in the suburbs. Beginning with the 1982 gubernatorial campaign, when his attack on Reaganomics was a central theme, Cuomo has frequently opposed Reagan Administration policies and has continued to relate national policy to state politics. Cuomo's address at the Democratic National Convention represented his most direct attack.

In 1985, Cuomo assumed a leadership role in opposing the Reagan Administration's proposal to eliminate the deduction for state and local taxes. The New York electorate was overwhelmingly opposed to the proposal and viewed it as particularly unfair to residents of New York State. An October 1985 MIPO statewide survey revealed both significant opposition across party lines to the Reagan tax proposal and an improved standing for Cuomo among Republicans for the leadership role he had assumed in national affairs (See Table 4.7).

Table 4.7

New York State Assessment of SALTD Proposal* and
Governor Cuomo's National Role

"One of the proposed changes in the tax system is the elimination of the tax deduction for state and local taxes. Do you favor or oppose such a change?"

	Favor	**Oppose**	**No Opinion**
New York State	16.9%	76.2%	6.9%
Party Identification			
Democrat	13.8%	81.5%	4.7%
Republican	19.0%	71.9%	9.0%
Independent	20.6%	74.1%	5.3%

"Do you feel that this proposal to simplify the tax system is as fair to New Yorkers as it is to residents of other states?"

	As Fair	**Not as Fair**	**Unsure**
New York State	18.7%	68.9%	12.4%
Party Identification			
Democrat	12.2%	80.6%	7.2%
Republican	27.1%	55.0%	17.9%
Independent	22.6%	65.6%	11.8%

Table 4.7 Continued

"I'm going to read you several statements about Governor Mario Cuomo. Please tell me if you agree or disagree with each one."

"Governor Cuomo is paying too much attention to national politics and not enough attention to New York State."

	Agree	**Disagree**	**No Opinion**
Republicans			
October 1985	38.8%	51.1%	10.2%
June 1985	46.7%	43.7%	9.5%

Source: MIPO, New York State survey, October 1985 and June 1985.

*Asked only of those who had heard or read about the tax reform proposal to eliminate state and local tax deductions.

Governor Cuomo was well positioned on this issue, and, to the degree that he defined the Reagan proposal as an attack on the middle class, he found a receptive audience in the New York suburbs. This was an issue of paramount significance for suburban homeowners (See Table 4.8). Cuomo asserted, "The people who take that deduction contribute 70% of the tax revenues to the United States. And who are these people?...87% of them are under $50,000. 50% of them are under $30,000. They are the heart and the soul of the middle class of Nassau, Suffolk, Westchester, and Rockland counties...and they get clobbered."[16]

Cuomo's initiatives in suburban politics have been based on his perception that the suburbs represent a far different political landscape than is assumed by conventional wisdom. This electorate is seen as selective and independent. Secretary to the Governor, Gerald Crotty, commented, "In terms of the kinds of backgrounds that you find in that area of the state and people paying attention to issues, you've got people...who stay

---

Table 4.8

New York Suburban Respondent's Assessments of the SALTD Proposal*

"One of the proposed changes in the tax system is the elimination of the tax deduction for state and local taxes. Do you favor or oppose such a change?"

	Favor	**Oppose**	**No Opinion**
New York Suburbs	18.3%	77.8%	3.8%

"Do you feel that this proposal to simplify the tax system is as fair to New Yorkers as it is to residents of other states?"

	As Fair	**Not as Fair**	**Unsure**
New York Suburbs	15.6%	72.8%	11.6%

*Asked only of those who had heard or read about the tax reform proposal to eliminate state and local tax deductions.

---

on top of issues, perhaps more so than other places, and people who are willing to keep an open mind."[17] Regarding the suburban voter, Cuomo elaborated, "They read more and they are politically independent...As for the suburbs, I think of them as thinking, eclectic, and discrete. I do not think of them as conservative or Republican."[18] So that, in the wake of the 1984 elections, Cuomo observed that this Democratic debacle did not constitute a conservative trend. "[The media] converted one headline into another. They converted the headline, 'Reagan Wins the Suburbs Big' into 'Conservatism Wins the Suburbs Big,' and it is two different things...I can win the suburbs. Anybody who believes the things I believe and makes them clear will win the suburbs."[19]

There is a two-way relationship between Mario Cuomo and the suburban voter. Not only does Governor Cuomo understand suburban political attitudes, but the suburban electorate perceives Mario Cuomo as a political leader whose approach is compatible with its own views. Cuomo's emphasis on government intervention into health care, housing, employment, and education, his compassion for the poor and the elderly, and his emphasis on family values closely match attitudes in the region. Tim Russert explained, "There is a responsive chord in the suburbs [to Cuomo] because the people you are communicating with have parents who are on Social Security, they bought their home through the G.I. Bill, and their sons and daughters are receiving student loans. There is a sense of responsiveness and responsibility there because, as much as they want to rail against big government and high taxes, once someone points out that they have been the beneficiaries of government programs and have probably achieved middle class and more because of the role of government, they don't reject you."[20]

In addition, although the suburban electorate may lack the details of Cuomo's legislative program, it is familiar with what Mario Cuomo represents ideologically, the approach he takes to government, and his value commitment. For the most part, slightly more than half of the electorate believes that Mario Cuomo is a "moderate" ideologically. Cuomo is viewed as a "liberal" by the next largest group of voters. Only a small group believes that Mario Cuomo is a political "conservative" (See Table 4.9). Democrats, Republicans, and Independents see Cuomo as a "moderate." Republicans are most likely to see him as left-of-center.

In terms of the ideology of the voter, liberals see Cuomo as either a "liberal" or a "moderate"; moderates see Cuomo as a "moderate"; and, conservatives divide among the categories. Combining the party and ideology of the voters further reveals their perception of Cuomo. The electorate consistently views Cuomo as either left-of-center or middle-of-the-road except for conservative-Democrats who view Cuomo as a conservative politically (See Table 4.9).

Table 4.9

Governor Cuomo's Ideological Rating and the New York Suburban
Respondent's Party Identification, Ideology, and Combined Ideological and
Party Identification

"Politically speaking, do you think that Governor Cuomo is a liberal, moderate, or
a conservative?"

	Liberal	**Moderate**	**Conservative**	**Unsure**
New York Suburbs	26.0%	51.3%	16.3%	6.4%
Party Identification				
Democrat	24.0%	54.9%	14.1%	7.0%
Republican	31.4%	44.2%	18.4%	5.9%
Independent	24.2%	55.1%	15.3%	5.4%
Ideology				
Liberal	41.6%	41.3%	9.7%	7.4%
Moderate	16.0%	69.0%	11.1%	4.0%
Conservative	34.8%	33.6%	26.4%	5.2%
Combined Ideological and Party Identification				
Liberal-Democrat	49.3%	42.7%	5.3%	2.7%
Moderate-Democrat	10.4%	75.4%	9.0%	5.2%
Conservative-Democrat	17.7%	23.3%	46.1%	12.9%
Liberal-Republican	41.1%	34.3%	13.2%	11.3%
Moderate-Republican	22.2%	63.9%	11.1%	2.8%
Conservative-Republican	40.1%	31.5%	25.0%	3.4%
Liberal-Independent	34.7%	43.3%	12.9%	9.2%
Moderate-Independent	15.6%	67.9%	12.4%	4.1%
Conservative-Independent	35.4%	39.1%	21.3%	4.2%

This group of conservative-Democrats is disproportionately
comprised of Catholic voters. Although some Catholics initially
adopted a wait-and-see attitude about Governor Cuomo, he
eventually gained their confidence through the position he took
on the traditional separation of church and state (See Table 4.10).
Suburban voters, including Catholics, overwhelmingly supported Cuomo's position as articulated at Notre Dame during the fall

85

of 1984. Columnist Mary McGrory wrote, "Cuomo boldly challenged Archbishop John J. O'Connor of New York...He questioned the archbishop's right to dictate how Catholics should vote...[Cuomo] warned fellow Catholics against imposing their views on a pluralistic society: 'We know the price of seeking to force our beliefs on others is that they might someday force theirs on us.' "[21]

Table 4.10

Comparison of Governor Cuomo's Performance Rating Between New York State Catholics and the New York State General Electorate*

	New York Catholics	New York Electorate
June 1985	69.6%	69.6%
September 1984	58.7%	66.1%
June 1984	58.1%	59.0%

*Source: MIPO New York State surveys.

Concerning Cuomo's approach to government and his value commitment, the analysis suggests that Cuomo is perceived in terms of the themes and values he has emphasized. For example, Governor Cuomo is seen by suburban voters as supporting an active government role in social policy. By a ratio of 3:1, the electorate believes that Mario Cuomo advocates government intervention into health care, housing, and employment. This is in contrast to a laissez-faire government role (See Table 4.11). Suburban voters believe by a ratio of 4:1 that Cuomo is especially sympathetic to the problems of the poor and the elderly. Similarly, Cuomo's emphasis on traditional family values is coming through to this electorate. Voters see Cuomo as advancing these values by more than 5:1 (See Table 4.11).

The New York Suburban Electorate and Mario Cuomo

What is especially noteworthy about voters' views of Mario Cuomo is that his approach to government's role is an important part of their perception of him. While many other Democrats have been reluctant to articulate these themes, Cuomo has become prominent by doing so. He has advocated a strong role for government in domestic policy balanced by an awareness of fiscal matters, saying society needs "a government that can give us both compassion and common sense in a single package...That [government] can take care of people in wheelchairs and the mentally ill and people who are poor without bankrupting fiscal [affairs]."[22]

Cuomo's ability to define the political agenda and present his approach to voters is further illustrated by the fact that although suburban voters see Cuomo as advocating an active government role in social policy and "as being especially sympathetic to the problems of the poor and the elderly," they do not see Cuomo as a "big spending liberal." Rather, they view him as someone who is "pragmatic and progressive" (See Table 4.11). In fact, this electorate believes that Cuomo's policies are fiscally sound. In addition, Cuomo has been able to attract diverse elements within the Democratic Party without appearing to be dominated by special interests. The suburban electorate believes that Cuomo is "independent of special interest groups" (See Table 4.11). As such, he has avoided the trap that has caught many other Democrats.

This analysis has identified that Mario Cuomo has strengthened his support to include the New York suburbs. Mario Cuomo understands the importance of the region and how his approach can be successful with this electorate. The suburban electorate, in turn, understands what Cuomo represents and rates him highly. The match which has resulted is between a political figure who draws upon both the old and the new and an electorate which has undergone a transformation also involving a mixture of the

Table 4.11

New York Suburban Respondent's Assessments of Governor Mario Cuomo

"I am now going to read to you a list of opposites. Please tell me which one best describes Governor Cuomo."

Government's Role

"He believes in active government intervention in health care, housing, and employment; or,	62.3%
He is reluctant to have government get involved in these areas."	20.4%
Both	2.0%
Neither	1.2%
Unsure	14.1%

Poor and Elderly

"He is especially sympathetic to the problems of the poor and the elderly; or,	76.6%
He is not particularly sympathetic to the poor and the elderly."	16.3%
Both	1.7%
Neither	1.2%
Unsure	4.2%

Spending

"He is a big spending liberal; or,	22.2%
He is pragmatic and progressive."	61.0%
Both	3.8%
Neither	3.5%
Unsure	9.6%

Special Interest Groups

"He is independent of special interest groups; or,	59.6%
He is controlled by special interest groups."	27.0%
Both	2.7%
Neither	2.0%
Unsure	8.6%

Table 4.11 Continued

"I'm now going to read to you several statements about Governor Mario Cuomo. Please tell me if you agree or disagree with each one."

	Agree	**Disagree**	**No Opinion**
"Governor Cuomo speaks on behalf of traditional family values."	78.1%	13.8%	8.1%
"Governor Cuomo's policies are fiscally sound."	65.3%	20.6%	14.1%

old and the new. Cuomo's views on government's role in social policy as articulated in his "family of New York" theme are at home with these voters. There is a compatibility between what he represents and an electorate which accepts his approach.

Cuomo offers updated statements of Democratic Party themes to an electorate which shies away from party affiliation. But because Cuomo is relatively new on the political scene, both his New York and national image escape traditional party labelling as occurred, for example, in 1984 with Walter Mondale. Because Cuomo skillfully presents a thematic and balanced approach and articulates his positions with consistency, he is not seen as a new and untested political figure like Gary Hart was in 1984. Cuomo communicates his views in a fresh way, yet he is familiar in substance.

Chapter Five

Implications for Political Analysis

"Gradually" is an overlooked word in political analysis. But it is a word which often captures the essence of what transpires in politics. This assessment of Mario Cuomo's political appeal in the suburbs has examined the development of the region over time and the trends which define its present political character. The suburbs have become a far different political landscape than was expected. The decline in the influence of political parties, the rise in Independent identification, the self-containment, diversity, and urbanization within the region, and the high socioeconomic characteristics of the population have created a new electorate. It is an electorate which exhibits a high interest in following politics and values the importance of issues when assessing political leaders and events. It is an electorate which brings great selectivity to politics. It is an electorate which views itself as moderate ideologically and which currently supports a positive government role in domestic policy.

This perspective on the political development of the suburbs helps to explain Mario Cuomo's popularity. But Cuomo's success as a politician in the suburbs was by no means guaranteed. Mario Cuomo has been able to address elements of both continuity and change which have shaped this electorate. He has blended a commitment to progressive attitudes on the role of government with an awareness of pragmatic concerns.

THE CUOMO FACTOR

In so doing, Mario Cuomo has successfully expanded the scope of his political support. He represents the concerns of the urban population which have traditionally been at the core of his party's support, and he has also broadened his appeal to include the new suburban electorate on the city's rim.

Evaluating electoral changes in the suburbs in the context of the region's development yields conclusions about how a political figure is perceived which are different from those of the realignment perspective which have dominated assessments of politics. Much political analysis in recent years has maintained that a realignment is occurring within the electorate involving a breakup of the traditional elements of the Democratic coalition and a shift to the right by the voters. There is a tension, however, between this interpretation of electoral trends and Mario Cuomo's popularity in the suburbs. The analysis of Cuomo's political appeal, in contrast to views which point to a political realignment to the GOP, suggests that the modification in party coalitions may be occurring—but not to the extent, not in the direction, and not for the reasons—that the realignment perspective maintains.

The concept of realignment posits that certain elections at the national level result in sharp and durable changes in the coalitional bases of politics throughout the entire party system. It assumes that although individual partisanship may be relatively stable over time, certain elections spark major changes in the overall composition of the political parties. These realigning elections establish the basis of political competition for several decades and define the issues over which that political competition takes place. Because the realignment perspective has dominated journalistic and political science accounts of voting behavior, this chapter examines the reliance upon the realignment approach to analyze politics and looks at the assertions upon which it is based.

Given the outcome of presidential contests since the New Deal, the focus of voting analyses has been on the splintering of the

Democratic Party and the emergence of the GOP as the new majority party. However, "If realignment is periodic, so is speculation about realignment—it follows every presidential election!"[1] Predictions about the demise of the Democratic coalition surfaced in 1946, following the death of Roosevelt and the GOP's recapture of the Congress after 14 years of Democratic control. As Kevin Phillips pointed out, "With the Eightieth Congress to reinforce their conviction that all would be well now that Roosevelt was dead, many Republican leaders looked forward to recapturing the White House in 1948. More than a few top Republicans wrote and spoke on how the normal Republicanism of the United States was about to reassert itself."[2] Similarly, in 1946, a post-election analysis described that "A new cycle in American political history is beginning. The 16 year hold of Democrats upon Congress is broken. Now begins a period of Republican power."[3]

The Democrats' despair was pervasive. Democratic Senator J. William Fulbright called for President Truman's resignation in light of GOP victories in congressional races. "President Truman should appoint a Republican Secretary of State and resign from office...[This] will place the responsibility of running the government on one party and prevent a stalemate that is likely to occur."[4] The dominance of the GOP was also illustrated by its control of the state houses in all but 13 states and its victories in 25 of 38 governorships outside the South and in 9 of 12 races in the East.

As 1948 approached, GOP chances were further enhanced by the disunity within the Democratic Party. As noted at the time, "The Democrats of many beliefs who were held together by Franklin D. Roosevelt for 12 years and through four presidential elections now are breaking apart. It took the master handling of Mr. Roosevelt, plus the emergencies of depression and war, to hold them together. With the outside pressures released and the strong hand of Mr. Roosevelt gone, internal disputes have taken over."[5] However, Truman was re-elected and the GOP failed to win the Congress. "The Democrats have swept all of Congress...recapturing the supposedly impregnable Republican House by a landslide and seizing firm control of the Senate," as *The New York Times* chronicled, "in one of the great political revolutions of American history."[6]

Although GOP hopes were dashed in that election, calls for the demise of the New Deal coalition and the imminent realignment of the electorate did not subside. The fifties brought renewed enthusiasm to GOP adherents based upon the growing affluence of the period and the belief that the Republican Party, which had long attracted the support of wealthier segments in society, would be the ongoing beneficiary of the postwar economic upturn. Following Eisenhower's election in 1952 and the Republican retaking of both Houses of Congress, Louis Harris, in *Is There A Republican Majority?*, looked at the breakup of the solid South and the presence of an enlarged white-collar group of voters as constituting the basis of a realignment in the direction of the Republican Party.[7]

The 1956 election was also interpreted in these terms. In referring to Eisenhower's re-election over Stevenson, James Reston wrote, "President Eisenhower produced a political revolution in the large cities of the North, fortress of Democratic strength for thirty years...this was the [New Deal] coalition General Eisenhower cracked for the first time in 1952 and broke wide open [in 1956]."[8]

By the end of the decade and into the 1960s, the Democrats had regained the White House and both Houses of Congress. In 1964, the Johnson landslide brought renewed calls of a realigning electorate. This time, however, the Democrats were seen as driving the Republicans into extinction. Angus Campbell, a leading pioneer in survey research, believed that the aftermath of 1964 would bring about a party realignment which would increase the prevailing Democratic advantage.[9]

Following the 1968 presidential election, however, analysis suggesting that the electorate was realigning towards the GOP resurfaced. Kevin Phillips wrote that 1968 marked the beginning of a new Republican cycle comparable in magnitude to the New Deal era.[10] The emerging majority was based on the vote total received by George Wallace and Richard Nixon. This represented, for Phillips, a new conservative majority to be housed in the GOP. Nixon's southern strategy in 1972 was seen as confirmation of this change in the electorate.[11] James Sundquist wrote that observers of presidential elections wondered if this was "the final breakup of the Roosevelt coalition" and the "beginning of a new cycle of Republican hegemony."[12]

The election of Jimmy Carter following Watergate was seen by some election analysts as re-assembling the traditional elements of the New Deal coalition. Subsequent analysis revealed that such an interpretation was misleading. Tom Wicker of *The New York Times* concluded that although Jimmy Carter restored the Democrats to power, he was not an heir to Roosevelt, but "the most conservative Democratic president since Grover Cleveland."[13]

The election of Ronald Reagan in 1980 once again brought calls that a realignment was in the works. Scammon and Wattenberg wrote, "So we come to 1980...what is important about the notion of political realignment is not that anyone can say 'It is here.' After all, other realignments were confirmable and noticeable only long after they occurred...No, what is important this year is that for the first time one can look at substantial evidence and say 'This has all the earmarks; it may turn out to be an ear.' "[14] Other commentators also looked at the 1980 election as the turning point in party politics. "It is plainly the end of an era," observed Theodore H. White on NBC News election night. Similarly, *The Washington Post* lead article following the election proclaimed, "Victorious Republicans and decimated Democrats looked back yesterday at an election that gave the national government its sharpest turn to the right in a generation and wondered if 1980 would go into the history books as the start of a new era of conservative and Republican dominance...Reagan cut deeply into both the blue-collar and southern wings of the old New Deal Democratic coalition as he carried 44 states and rolled up 51% of the popular vote in a three-man race."[15]

Soon after the 1984 landslide, the realignment arguments reappeared. One election analyst began, "President Reagan begins his second term with a historic opportunity to turn the Republicans into a majority party that could dominate American politics for decades."[16] Benjamin Ginsberg and Martin Shefter also assessed President Reagan's re-election in realignment terms. They stated, "potentially more important than Reagan's margin of victory was his ability to consolidate and reinforce an alliance among traditionally Republican and traditionally Democratic voting blocs. If this coalition were to endure, it would mark the end of one era in American politics and the beginning of a new one—that is, a critical realignment."[17]

Although the realignment perspective has been used extensively during recent decades, problems exist with the orientation. Difficulties arise from both the limitations of the framework and the assumptions upon which it is based. As has been noted, "American voting patterns are a kaleidoscope of sociology, history, geography, and economics. Of course, the threads are very tangled and complex, but they can be pulled apart. Once the correct framework has been erected, national voting patterns can be structured, explained, correlated, and predicted to a surprising degree. The trick is to build the framework."[18]

The realignment perspective has failed to be predictive and has been overly relied upon by academicians who first introduced it, and journalists who have frequently applied it. The difficulty stems from the inability to know with certainty at any one time that a realignment is occurring because a central characteristic of a realignment is its durability. As a result, realignment theories tend to be much more disorderly than is generally thought. The political science literature is also unclear as to how the concept of realignment should be approached. Although scholarship deals with the characteristics of a realignment, it fails to specify exactly what it is. Because the theories are not sufficiently articulated and lack precision and detail, there are no reliable indices upon which to measure and determine what is occurring in the electorate at any one point in time, and certainly, what the future implications of a trend are going to be. So, what the next realignment would look like, if it occurs, remains in doubt. As Clubb critiqued the use of realignment theories, "Much of this discussion has occurred without clear conceptualizations of the realignment process, clear ideas of realigning electoral change, or an effective means to assess and measure such change."[19] These theories fail to meet one of the cardinal rules of social science: criteria should be made so explicit that when trying to match theory with reality, "You know it when you see it."

Projections about impending realignments have depended upon three measures: the outcome of an election, a change in the gap separating Democratic and Republican party identification, and an ideological swing among large numbers of voters. However, reliance upon these indicators has often resulted in misleading claims.

First, election outcomes, as discussed in the review of presidential elections since the New Deal, have been used as a measure of party dominance and as the basis of realignment projections. Yet, election data of this sort is extremely limited in assessing anything beyond the "what" of politics to include the "how" or the "why." James Sundquist noted, "If there are many realigning forces at work simultaneously...the analysis of election data alone does little to help untangle them...Election data, by compressing into a single set of figures the consequences of all the causative factors that may be in operation on a given November Tuesday, can be positively misleading...."[20]

The inadequacy of election outcomes as the basis of realignment projections is further compounded by changes which have occurred in the technology of campaigns and in the electorate's assessments of candidates. Significant agreement exists among political scientists and journalists, for example, over the growing influence of television on politics. This trend places a higher premium on the personality of the candidates as portrayed by the media during a campaign and other short-term factors, such as issues which emerge, a flaw in strategy, or a slip during a televised debate. Political analysts must recognize the role played by these elements in determining election winners and losers because, as John Petrocik has pointed out, these factors can cause elections to take on characteristics that mistakenly lead one to believe that a realignment has occurred. "If a definition of realignment that turns on the results of an election is not adequate, there is some reason to believe that an emphasis on election statistics to identify a realignment will also not always be adequate."[21] For voting analysts, inferring realigning patterns in the electorate based upon election outcomes and related data in an era marked by candidate and media oriented politics is a risky business.

Furthermore, the use of election outcomes as the basis of a realignment has focused primarily on presidential races, where the GOP has dominated, thereby overlooking the continued successes of Democrats for other offices. Compare the GOP position in 1952 with its strength following the 1984 elections. In 1952, Republicans held 221 seats in the House to 183 in 1984; 30 of 48 governorships to 16 of 50; and, both houses in 26 of 47 state legislatures as compared to 11 of 49 following the 1984 election. The GOP was even in the Senate compared with a narrow majority, and Eisenhower had just won with 55% of the vote to 59% for Reagan. All in all, Republicans held approximately 25% of the nation's elected offices at a time when speculation about the breakup of the Democrats and a realignment to the GOP was high.

Second, changes in party identification have also been used to assess party realignments. As the gap in the number of Democrats and Republicans narrows, calls labelling the trend a "realignment" often surface. Party identification emerged as a core concept in political science in the 1950s, largely as the result of the work of scholars at the University of Michigan. In the ensuing decades, these and other researchers analyzed voting behavior in terms of voters' attachments to a political party. These theories suggest that most voters possess relatively stable sets of attitudes and predispositions about politics and political parties. According to Paul Kleppner, these attitudes emerge from early childhood socialization experiences, are reinforced by subsequent group involvements, and are resistant to change. "Chief among these stable predispositions is the individual's 'affective orientation' to a political party. It is that underlying sense of psychological identification with a particular party, that internalized sense of 'being' a Democrat or a Republican, that imparts long-term consistency to the individual's voting decision."[22] As a result, party identification allows the two parties to serve as standard setting groups for large numbers of voters.

Great political significance has been attached to the proportion of voters who align with one party or another and, more importantly, to any changes in that alignment. Following land-slides, party identification has often fluctuated, and the gap separating the major parties has changed. This has led to mistaken conclusions about long-term party realignment. For example, after Eisenhower's re-election in 1956, the Democratic edge over the GOP narrowed. *Time* reported soon thereafter that the GOP had closed the gap and had carved extensive inroads into Democratic support.[23] In the fall of 1972, with Republican incumbent Richard Nixon well on his way to a landslide re-election and the Democratic Party acting like a majority party in disarray, party identification figures revealed a Republican surge. Pollster Albert Sindlinger found that the Democratic lead over the GOP had shrunk from 15% in July 1972 to 4% in September.[24]

Fueled by Reagan's victories and changes in party identifica-tion, speculation of an impending realignment has abounded. In 1981, during Reagan's first year in office, national surveys revealed an erosion in the Democrats' lead over the Republi-cans in party identification. Sundquist wrote that the data from this period produced "a flurry of newspaper speculation about a Reagan realignment...the Gallup Poll showed a Republican gain of 7% points between early 1980 and early 1981, comprising a 6 point loss by the Democrats and a 1 point drop of self-declared Independents."[25] *The New York Times* pointed out that although Democrats still outnumbered Republicans, the lead was only half what it was when the presidential campaign of 1980 had commenced the previous year. "The changes within the electorate...offer the Republicans an opportunity to effect a classic political realignment comparable to the Democratic accession to power in the 1930s."[26] Adam Clymer and Kathleen Frankovic wrote at the time, "These new Republicans are the flesh on the bone of polling figures that record what may be the most important political development in half a century: the Republican realignment. It has not happened yet, but may be developing. If the realignment materializes, it will transform a minority party that sometimes wins big into the dominant political party in the United States."[27] Following Reagan's re-election in 1984, polls again identified a closing gap between the Democratic and Republican parties, and analysis focused on party realignment. The Gallup Poll showed that Republican identification had climbed to a three decade high, and the gap separating the two major parties had closed to only 4%.[28]

There are several difficulties in drawing far-reaching conclusions about electoral trends based upon these changes in party identification. Even in an era of strong partisanship, such as was the case until the 1960s, inferences based upon the changing gap in party identification were not reliable. During the height of the Roosevelt Administration, voters who identified with the Democratic Party did not always exceed those who identified with the Republican Party. In 1940, the electorate was divided: 40% Republican and 39% Democratic.[29] Similarly, in 1944, at the time of Roosevelt's fourth election to the presidency, the Gallup Poll reported that the electorate still remained split, with 41% seeing themselves as Democrats and 39% calling themselves Republicans. Analysis about the long-term political significance of these statistics would have been misleading. In addition, despite short-term ups and downs in party identification, a comparison of the ratio of Democrats to Republicans from 1952 through 1980, for example, reveals very little change in the electorate with the exception of 1964. Throughout this period, there were about three Democrats to every two Republicans,

In the current political climate with its weakened partisanship, analysis based upon party identification is even more suspect. The present period is characterized by a decline in voter identification in both political parties. As William Crotty pointed out, "Fewer people are identifying with either of the political parties, and even among those who do, the intensity of their identification is falling off markedly...As party identification has declined in importance, the number and significance of Independent voters has increased substantially. In return, the unpredictability and volatility of the vote returns attest to the weakening of party ties and the decline of party loyalty."[30]

In this light, analysis of the realignment potential of today's electorate must be made cautiously. Instead of reflecting a realigning trend, a narrowing in the gap separating the two parties has frequently been followed by a re-widening. Changes in party identification seem to be increasingly linked, like election outcomes, to short-term phenomena. For example, following the 1980 presidential election, Republicans hoped that Ronald Reagan would forge a new coalition two years after taking office and would duplicate for the GOP what Roosevelt had done for the Democrats. But the analogy to the elections of 1932 and 1934 did not materialize. In the spring of 1982, the Gallup Poll revealed that only 28% of the respondents called themselves Republicans, unchanged from the previous year. However, in relative terms the GOP lost ground, for the Democrats had gained four points at the expense of the Independents, rising from 41% to 45%. By June, the Republicans slipped to 26% while the Democrats rose to 48%. Other national polls showed a comparable halt to the Republican advance and the beginnings of a retreat.[31] Sundquist has observed that these figures do not "reflect anything approaching the monumental gains and losses in party affiliation that occurred during the major realignment of the 1930s."[32]

After the Reagan 1984 landslide, a narrowing of the gap separating the major parties recurred. Not unlike 1981, this was followed by a re-widening of the distance separating the number of Democrats and Republicans. This time, the separation has re-emerged without the assistance of the recession which had contributed to Democratic gains in 1982. According to ABC News/*Washington Post* polls, from January 1985 to March 1985, "the Democrats came from 1 percentage point behind to 10 percentage points ahead of the Republicans. A less detailed poll...suggests that the trend favoring the Democrats was continuing. The Gallup Poll found that for the entire first quarter of the year, the Republican Party had achieved near-parity with the Democratic Party...[However] Democrats appeared to be again gaining strength by March."[33] In early 1986, the CBS News/*New York Times* poll showed that the distance separating the Democrats and Republicans was similar to January 1981, when Reagan first assumed office. They concluded that President Reagan was not making much further progress in turning his party into the majority.[34] Republican hopes for a realignment of the parties and the creation of a new Republican majority have not been fulfilled.[35]

Shifting gaps in party identification have been of questionable meaning historically and are even less significant in the current political climate. The character of electoral politics today is associated with rising Independent identification, greater volatility in voters' preferences, and fewer traditional party dominated choices. Given these trends, it becomes necessary to ask how useful party identification is as a concept to analyze the electorate, and how much reliance should be placed upon changing identification between the Democrats and the Republicans.

An alternative interpretation of this view of the electorate has been developed in recent years. The perspective has been advanced that the electorate has been experiencing a dealignment, not a realignment. This concept of dealignment has gained popularity among some political scientists, but has yet to take hold, for the most part, in journalistic analyses of elections.

Dealignment emerges from the observation that not since the New Deal have so many voters been floating free of their traditional political party moorings. Rather than characterizing present trends in the electorate as a realignment between parties, although there are some changes occurring, the more dominant phenomenon involves voters moving away from political parties altogether.[36] Voting is less sharply defined along partisan lines. Kevin Phillips now believes that the current volatility in the electorate suggests an "electoral no-man's land" of dealignment. He notes that within this broader trend short-term party gains can still take place, but that the expected realignment did not occur.[37]

Party dealignment is illustrated by an increase in Independent identification, a weakening of party ties among partisan identifiers, and a rise in split-ticket voting. William Schneider has suggested that these trends represent a classic pattern of dealignment where no party approaches a clear cut majority.[38] From this dealignment perspective, Ladd and Hadley have concluded, "Important facets of the contemporary partisan transformation simply do not comprise the movement of groups of voters from one party to another. The claims of any party, present or future, to majority status are blocked by the long-term weakening of popular partisan attachments. To a greater extent than ever before, the American electorate is candidate and issue oriented rather than party oriented."[39] Party identification may still occupy an important place in American politics, but not to the degree necessary for a party realignment.

A third factor often used to measure a party realignment involves an ideological shift in the electorate. In the current political climate, the electorate is often seen as swinging dramatically to the right, deserting the view that government should play an active role in domestic policy. From this perspective, a conservative majority housed in the Republican

Party is emerging. The crushing defeat of liberal George McGovern, the fracturing of the Democratic Party during the 1970s, and the success of Ronald Reagan have all been advanced as evidence of this trend. Reflecting this view, it was noted in 1980 that "for the Democratic Party these are hardly the best of times...Its ranks are divided, perhaps irreconcilably, by a bitter feud that is personal as well as ideological. Worst of all, its traditionally liberal call to arms on behalf of the poor, the jobless, and the dispossessed sounds increasingly out of tune in a nation drifting slowly rightward."[40] Similarly, Reagan's re-election in 1984 was proclaimed as a furthering of this conservative trend and was seen as a "mandate for continuation of his conservative policies from voters all across America."[41]

Evidence of conservative movement characterizing a realignment, however, has been sketchy. Walter Dean Burnham wrote that with regard to Reagan's vote in 1980 an "exceptional proportion of voters floated from one candidate to another: the break of many of them toward Reagan near the very end made the presidential outcome a much more decisive Republican victory than most had anticipated."[42] This election is seen as a landslide vote of no confidence in an incumbent administration rather than a conservative swing ideologically in the electorate. Only 11% of the voters chose Reagan because "he is a real conservative," an ideological basis, whereas 38% of Reagan backers cited "it's time for a change" as the basis of their vote.[43]

Election day polling data in 1984 also pointed out that ideological and policy preferences were not the basis of voters' decisions, but rather the personalities of the candidates and pocketbook issues were determining.[44] Voter preference for Ronald Reagan based on his being the "real conservative," a limited factor in 1980, fell to only 6% among Reagan supporters in 1984.[45] Had Reagan campaigned more on a conservative platform in this election, then analyses which interpreted his victory in ideological terms would have made more sense. Polls revealed, however, a substantial gap between Reagan's support and his stands on policy issues, and *The New York Times* survey concluded that Reagan had failed to obtain a policy mandate.[46]

Furthermore, although Walter Mondale was considered a liberal-Democrat, he did not emphasize a liberal-Democratic message. Despite George Will's contention that Mondale's defeat "buried the most ideologically uniform and liberal ticket in American history,"[47] the Mondale-Ferraro ticket advocated lowered deficits, increased taxes, and higher military spending. As *U.S. News and World Report* noted, "Walter Mondale and Geraldine Ferraro, hitting the campaign trail together for the first time, trumpeted themes that were right out of Ronald Reagan's 1980 election book. The two Democrats delivered pitches on family values, fiscal responsibility, and crime fighting...[Voters] heard little from either ticket mate about spending more money on social and domestic programs—a traditional Democratic campaign stance."[48] Mondale saw this platform as a repositioning of the Democratic Party away from a more liberal stance. "If a few years ago you had said our party would come out more strongly than the (GOP) for reducing the debt, that we would come out for real defense growth of 4%, that we would have a platform with no major new programs, most people would have said that can't possibly be. I'm proud of the fact that I've moved our party...into something realistic and practical."[49]

It was only a late fall redirection in strategy that resulted in the changed emphasis in the Mondale campaign. The shift in themes called attention to Reagan's ties to right-wing evangelical leaders, his policies in Central America, his hopes of stacking the Supreme Court with anti-abortion conservatives, and his opposition to the Equal Rights Amendment. This shift by

Mondale was seen as a strategic effort that "blunts the issue of the federal budget deficit and focuses on broader social and foreign policy themes."[50] By that point, however, Mondale was seen as being indecisive and tied to special interest groups. His running mate was already entangled with accountants and bishops.[51]

Rather than turning on some ideological criteria, the outcome of the 1984 election was based on the voters' sense that President Reagan had done a good job and deserved to be re-elected. William Schneider has argued that people were voting in 1980 not for conservatism but for change, and in 1984, the electorate chose neither conservatism nor change, but continuity. He wrote, "The fact that both elections were decided on the basis of performance rather than ideology is surprising only because Reagan is such an ideological figure. His achievement in 1980 was to win the support of many voters who did not agree with him ideologically. He did it again [in 1984]."[52] President Reagan's continued popularity seems to be more of a comment on the state of the economy and positive feelings toward him personally than about long-term ideological and policy directions.

This interpretation is consistent with the view in political science that points to voters' retrospective judgments of performance as determining the outcomes of presidential races.[53] From this perspective, the electorate comes to either reject or accept the incumbent seeking re-election based on short-term assessments of him. These evaluations may include pocketbook issues, so that in 1980, Jimmy Carter can be seen as increasingly beset by economic difficulties which led to a clear rejection of his Administration. As Seymour Martin Lipset wrote, "since the election turned on a vote against a 'failed' administration rather than a positive choice between alternative orientations, it is impossible to say that a realignment—the creation of a new long-term Republican majority—has occurred."[54] In 1984, incumbent President Reagan was the beneficiary of a similar process of voters' evaluations. Long-term realignment is unlikely if short-term economic fluctuation dominates voters' behavior.

An ideological shift in the electorate is central to realignment theory, but the view that the electorate has swung dramatically to the right, thereby foretelling a realignment, is open to question. While there has been a conservative shift in policy, there remains an ongoing commitment on the part of the electorate to maintain the thrust of government initiatives into domestic policy. There is little evidence, for example, that popular sentiment has turned against the domestic programs of the New Deal or the Great Society. Surveys by *The New York Times* and *The Washington Post* have also shown that "very few Americans wished to roll back any of the social programs initiated by the New Deal and its political progeny—the Fair Deal, New Frontier, and Great Society. By wide margins, the public continues to support Social Security, Medicare, aid to education, desegregation of schools, housing, employment, public accommodations, and the ballot box."[55]

Throughout 1980, surveys showed that voters also opposed sizeable cuts in spending for health, education, and related services. Although Reagan cutback proposals enjoyed substantial support in Congress immediately following his election, the CBS News/*New York Times* survey revealed little public enthusiasm for these reductions. The poll indicated that "only 25% of those polled supported cutting federal aid to college students and 24% favored cutting aid for the unemployed. And only 18% favored reductions in antipollution spending, 17% cuts in mass transit aid and 16% reduced spending for highways... Food stamps [was] the exception...but even so there [were] as many Americans who want[ed] food stamp spending kept the same or increased as there [were] those who want[ed] it cut."[56]

By the summer of 1981, almost half the electorate thought that the cuts enacted during the legislative session had gone too far, and only 19% thought that they should go farther.[57]

Public support for spending for domestic programs has continued throughout the 1980s in the face of numerous cuts in social programs and plans for far deeper cuts by the Reagan Administration. Public opinion polls have shown that the number of those who think President Reagan has gone too far in trying to cut back government social programs has exceeded the number who feel that Reagan has not gone far enough. An ABC News/*Washington Post* poll found that only one third of the electorate favored substantial cuts in social programs to reduce the deficit, although nearly two-thirds believed that such cuts were going to be made.[58] The trend in public opinion is against any further reductions. The CBS News/*New York Times* poll shortly after the 1984 election found that when compared to a 1980 post-election survey, "There is no suggestion in this poll that the American public has grown more conservative during the four years of the Reagan Administration. If anything, there is more willingness now to spend money on domestic programs and a better assessment of the social programs of the 1960s."[59]

In addition, the public increasingly supports a re-prioritization away from defense toward social program spending. Regarding the national budget, only 39% approve of social spending cuts, whereas 66% want defense expenditures trimmed to reduce the deficit.[60] Furthermore, an ABC News/*Washington Post* survey indicated that the average person believes that the government wastes 42¢ of every tax dollar and, by two to one, people see more waste coming from defense than from social programs. "Fifty percent of the people interviewed see more waste in military spending, 28% see more in social programs. The rest think it is a toss-up between the two."[61]

The question of a shift towards conservatism was the subject of a CBS News/*New York Times* follow-up poll to data collected at the beginning of the Reagan Administration. "The responses showed no consistent evidence of change, certainly not in a conservative direction. About as many people believe now as they did five years ago, for example, that the government should see to it that everyone has a good job and a good standard of living. Fewer people think that welfare recipients could get along without welfare payments. Fewer people believe that government creates more problems than it solves. More people feel that the poverty programs of the 1960s made things better...Even more significantly, perhaps, fully 66% think the government should spend money now on efforts similar to those of the Great Society programs to help the poor people in the United States."[62] The report suggests that although President Reagan continues to be extremely popular, "there is no clear evidence that he has yet achieved the ideological realignment he has long sought."[63]

If there is a trend toward conservatism, it has been subtle and is not evidence of a changing public ideology. Most Americans remain "operational liberals" favoring a wide range of governmental programs and policies.[64] As William Flanigan and Nancy Zingale summarized, "In economic matters Americans are more liberal than conservative. Increased government activity in domestic economic affairs or in welfare programs elicits no wide-spread, consistent public opposition...the ideological opponents of government activity are not numerous in the general public. In this respect, as in many others, the substantial number of political leaders, including President Reagan, who oppose 'liberal' domestic economic programs is not a reflection of public opinion."[65] A poll conducted for the Heritage Foundation found that 75% of the nation believes that welfare benefits are about right or should be raised. More than 73% of those questioned said people receiving aid really need the help to get by.[66]

Voters' attitudes on government priorities differ nonetheless from the positions of most candidates of both parties, and certainly, from the views of the more conservative oriented ones. To understand the relationship between voters' views and electoral success, analysts must take into account momentum and leadership. Despite liberal attitudes expressed by the public in opinion surveys, there has been a revival of the conservative agenda. Conservative viewpoints have defined discussion during the past decade on inflation, economic recessions, the standard of living, and levels of government spending. The solutions which have been advanced by members of both parties closely resemble traditional Republican Party stances and have included cutting taxes, restricting government spending, balancing the budget, tightening the money supply, and trimming social welfare programs. In this context, Democratic candidates have often failed to present an alternative program, and liberal answers have been on the defensive. But these poll results point out that public attitudes run counter to the views of many Democrats who believe that there is no longer any political mileage in advocating for federal domestic programs.[67]

Interpreting the elections of the period requires emphasizing, as William Crotty pointed out, "the changing nature of politics in the last decade [more] than any pronounced shift in voter attitudes. It is true that conservative issues dominated political debate. It is also clear that conservative groups and causes became better organized...Whereas liberal assumptions and programs appeared under sustained attack, the conservative movement was buoyed...."[68] As potent as the issues of the conservatives have been in shaping political dialogue, they have lacked the power within the electorate to replace the New Deal party system with a new one organized on a different rationale and with a changed definition of party conflict. The issues advanced by the conservatives are insufficient to redefine party life. None is of the magnitude of slavery, free silver, or the hardships of the Depression.[69] As a result, conflicts over the role of government in alleviating social distress and regulating the economy are the same today as those that structured political debate during the 1930s.

Despite numerous GOP electoral successes, particularly at the presidential level, some narrowing of the gap in party identification, and greater dominance of the political agenda by conservative approaches, these trends have not resulted in the often projected realignment. Although changes in the electorate and in the political process require adaptation on the part of candidates and parties, the old alignment and its issues still carry significant weight with voters until a new alignment is effectuated. As Clubb noted, "The issues, symbols, and voter coalitions produced by the preceding realignment retain salience and importance for the electorate. To ignore them is to risk defeat at the polls."[70] Warned by some party leaders as long ago as 1946 against swinging to the right and becoming "the conservative little brother of the Republicans,"[71] Democratic candidates have often been reluctant to provide leadership to advance their party's philosophy and to articulate themes consistent with it. This has cost them severely at the polls in recent years.

Although less conservative attitudes remain central in today's electorate, they do not dominate political dialogue, and voters have sought out new candidates and parties. A constituency exists, though largely ignored, in favor of continued government intervention into domestic policy. These attitudes are reflected in nationwide data and in the New York suburbs. The national pattern suggests, furthermore, that the New York suburban picture is not atypical. This region's voters are in step with the national electorate.

It is within this context that Mario Cuomo has emerged on

the political scene. Cuomo is not a political anomaly in an otherwise realigning trend toward the GOP, nor is he merely a dealignment media centered political figure. Rather, his appeal is based upon his ability to define the political agenda and to present substantive themes which are important to today's voters. The Cuomo Factor, as advanced in this analysis, makes clear that by taking a forceful position on government involvement in domestic policy, combined with a pragmatic view of government's role, Mario Cuomo presents the electorate with a thematic approach which is both consistent with his party's values and compatible with contemporary views of the voters. In so doing, Cuomo has established a political appeal which has maintained his party's urban base of support while reaching out to suburban voters. The Cuomo Factor recalls the "echo chamber" view of V.O. Key. "...The people's verdict [on candidates and parties] can be no more than a selective reflection from among the alternatives and outlooks presented to them."[72]

The realignment perspective is misleading to the degree that it has focused attention on an expected upheaval of the electorate in the direction of the GOP based upon election outcomes, a change in party identification, and a movement in public opinion in a more conservative direction. In contrast, the Mario Cuomo experience in New York, as well as this nationwide data on these realignment issues, demonstrate that: a more gradual change in the electorate is occurring as voters become less party oriented and increasingly selective; the electorate is far less conservative on issues of public policy than is generally thought; and, candidates of both political parties have the potential to broaden their appeal to suburban voters who support government's commitment to domestic policy. This analysis suggests that a political appeal, emphasizing a positive role for government, is attractive to large numbers of voters. That is what Mario Cuomo has demonstrated in the New York suburbs.

THE CUOMO FACTOR

Concerning Mario Cuomo's political future, whether Cuomo's ties to these suburban voters will be long lasting remains unknown. Whether Cuomo will benefit from this political trend in the presidential campaign of 1988 or beyond remains to be seen. Cuomo has attracted substantial national attention and support, but he will have to demonstrate that he can amass the organizational resources necessary to launch such a national effort. As Carl Leubsdorf of *The Dallas Morning News* commented, "You have got to be on the track once. Most presidential candidates get to try out their act in obscurity. Cuomo does not have that luxury...He is going to have to be good from the start...It comes down to the experience of the candidate, the staff, and the operation."[73]

Cuomo will also have to overcome some timetable restrictions to be a presidential candidate in 1988. He has often commented on the impracticality of running for re-election as governor one year and then turning around and running a presidential campaign the following year. "I think as a practical matter...if you are running for governor, how the heck do you turn around and run for president?...I say, 'Show me the calendar. Show me how you do it.' It doesn't work that way."[74] On this point, Carl Leubsdorf noted, "The question is how quickly after '86 could he start working on '88 and make it look credible. The longer he waits, the more trouble he has...Cuomo has to be in from the start."[75]

Furthermore, Cuomo will have to respond, as he did successfully during his 1986 re-election campaign, to the criticism that his rhetoric is not matched by his accomplishments. On this point, Cuomo argues, "What about the biggest tax cut in [New York] history. What about the biggest rebuilding New York bond issue in history. What about the first generally accepted accounting principle budget. What about the enormous victory over Washington on the disallowance of deductability. What about the biggest environmental budget in history. What about the 850,000 more people at work. [Critics say that] I did not focus on one thing. If I had said nothing but let's rebuild New York, and identified myself over and over with that, then I could have gotten an award for the big rebuilding program. But I don't want to do it that way. If by doing too much, I don't get credit for doing enough, I'll settle for that."[76]

Most significantly, in assessing his political future, Cuomo must decide whether he will continue to emphasize nationally the approach he has established in New York State. In analyzing Cuomo's 1986 budget message, Maurice Carroll, former Albany bureau chief of *The New York Times,* noted that Cuomo's "Work, Not Welfare" proposal represented an altered tone for Cuomo. Referring to Cuomo's statement a year earlier that "The Future Once Happened Here," Carroll noted that Cuomo had stirred memories of Alfred E. Smith and Franklin D. Roosevelt. "Everyone applauded. They knew that what began in Albany under Governor Smith had been honed and then expanded into the New Deal by President Roosevelt, starting a half-century of liberal social legislation. Earlier this month...Mr. Cuomo said, 'Work is better than Welfare.' It was a considerable change, both in the Governor's tone and in the sentiments...Mr. Cuomo, who has hailed the birth of the New Deal here in Albany...was sounding a traditionally conservative theme. He did not limit it to welfare...[Cuomo stated], 'I'm not anxious to see the state do things the private sector does better.'"[77]

If Cuomo decides to run for president, he will also have to avoid getting embroiled in disputes, which have even blemished his landslide re-election, and rely instead on the approach that has been effective for him in New York and brought him national acclaim, as well. Cuomo must be perceived nationally, as he is in New York, as a progressive and pragmatic force for government involvement. Regardless of whether Cuomo enters the presidential sweepstakes, his success makes clear that there is a viable political appeal to today's suburban voters which emphasizes a positive role for government in domestic policy. It is an approach which others could take up as well in post-Reagan America.

[1]Robin Herman, "The Upstate Campaign: Voter Apathy and Pride," *The New York Times,* August 27, 1982, pg. B1.

[2]David Hepp, *Inside Albany,* August 28, 1982.

[3]David S. Broder, "Meet Mario Machiavelli," *The Washington Post National Weekly,* August 6, 1984, pg. 4.

[4]Michael Oreskes, "Cuomo at Mid-term: The Governor's Reputation is Based on Words More than Deeds," *The New York Times,* January 7, 1985, pg. B1.

[5]Mario Cuomo, *Inside Albany,* July 5, 1985.

[6]Albert Hunt, "Mario Cuomo: Star Rising in the East," *The Wall Street Journal,* May 31, 1983, pg. 28E.

[7]David Langdon quoted in Michael Oreskes, "Cuomo's Personal Touch," *The New York Times Magazine,* January 29, 1984, pg. 33. David Langdon, then Counselor to former New York State Assembly Speaker Stanley Fink.

[8]Marc Humbert, *Inside Albany,* July 5, 1985.

[9]Interview with Timothy Russert, February 20, 1986.

[10]Mario Cuomo, Speech before the AFL-CIO Convention, Kiamesha Lake, New York, August 31, 1982. *Diaries of Mario M. Cuomo: The Campaign for Governor* (New York: Random House, 1984).

[11]Sidney Schanberg, "Will the Best Man Win?" *The New York Times,* July 10, 1982, pg. A23.

[12]Maurice Carroll, "Four in Contest for Carey's Post Wind Up Drives," *The New York Times,* September 22, 1982, pg. B4.

[13]Michael Kramer, "Lew Lehrman's $7-Million Education," *New York,* September 27, 1982, pg. 28.

[14]*New York Post* Gubernatorial Debate, October 7, 1982.

[15]Michael Oreskes, "Cuomo Assails Tax Plan," *The New York Times,* October 14, 1982, pg. B11.

[16]David Garth quoted in Kramer, *op. cit.*

[17]Jane Perlez, "Aide Says Reagan Visit for Lehrman is Unlikely," *The New York Times,* September 28, 1982, pg. B3.

[18]*Ibid.*

[19]Frank Lynn, "Dominance of Joblessness as Issue Helping Cuomo in Governor Race," *The New York Times,* October 20, 1982, pg. A1.

[20]George Will, *This Week with David Brinkley,* October 1982.

[21]Frank Lynn, *op. cit.*

[22]CBS News Surveys, November 2, 1982 as reported in *Public Opinion,* December/January 1983, pg. 38.

23Marist Institute for Public Opinion, Marist College, Election Day Exit Poll, 1982.

24Mario Cuomo, *Diaries,* pp. 3, 457.

25*Ibid.,* pg. 7.

26Joyce Purnick, "Joyous Cuomo Grateful for Support from Koch," *The New York Times,* September 24, 1982, pg. B6.

27Joe Klein, "The Meaning of Mario," *New York,* June 14, 1982, pg. 36.

28Frank Lynn, "Cuomo Win Sets the Stage for a Classic, Classy Duel," *The New York Times,* September 26, 1982, pg. E6.

29Michael Oreskes, "Analysts Feel Cuomo Won the Old-Fashioned Way," *The New York Times,* September 25, 1982, pg. A31.

30*New York Post* Gubernatorial Debate.

31Mario Cuomo, *Diaries,* pg. 6; see also "Lackawanna Blues," *The New York Times,* May 21, 1983, pg. 23.

32Lewis Lehrman, *Inside Albany,* October 30, 1982.

33Mario Cuomo, *Inside Albany,* October 30, 1982.

34Frank Lynn, "A Clash of Ideologies in the Campaign for Governor," *The New York Times,* October 12, 1982, pg. B4.

35Interview with Lars-Erik Nelson, July 31, 1986.

36Mario Cuomo, "Inaugural Address," Albany, New York, January 1, 1983.

37*Ibid.*

38Mario Cuomo, "State of the State," Albany, New York, January 5, 1983.

39Michael DelGuidice quoted in Michael Oreskes, "Cuomo's First Budget: A Mixture of Give and Take," *The New York Times,* February 1, 1983, pg. B4.

40Mario Cuomo, Keynote Speech at the 1984 Democratic National Convention, San Francisco, Calif., July 16, 1984.

41Gerald Pomper, *The Election of 1984: Reports and Interpretations* (Chatham, NJ: Chatham House Publishers, Inc., 1985) pg. 87.

42Mario Cuomo, "State of the State," Albany, New York, January 9, 1985.

43Mario Cuomo, "E Pur Si Muove," Yale University, New Haven, Connecticut, February 15, 1985.

44*Ibid.*

45Mario Cuomo, "Abraham Lincoln and Our 'Unfinished Work,' " Address before the Abraham Lincoln Association, Springfield, Illinois, February 12, 1986.

46David Hepp, *Inside Albany,* February 15, 1986.

[47]David S. Broder, "Democrats: Two Voices of Hope," *The Washington Post National Weekly,* March 18, 1985, pg. 4.

[48]Jeffrey Schmalz, "Cuomo Aims Sharp Attack At Reagan," *The New York Times,* April 23, 1986, pg. B1.

[49]Andrew O'Rourke quoted in Frank Lynn, "O'Rourke, of Westchester, Enters Governor's Race," *The New York Times,* April 17, 1986, pg. 1.

[50]*Ibid.*

[51]Mario Cuomo, selected campaign literature, June 1986.

[52]Unless otherwise noted, a job performance rating or approval rating refers to the combined "excellent" and "good" scores on a four point scale. The four categories are "excellent," "good," "fair," and "poor."

Footnotes for Chapter Two

[1]The term New York Suburbs refers to the four counties within New York State considered to be part of the suburban ring surrounding New York City. These include Nassau and Suffolk counties on Long Island, and Westchester and Rockland counties to the city's north.

[2]It should be recognized that suburban communities in upstate New York have also experienced similar trends. See Jeffrey Stonecash "An Eroding Base?"*Empire State Report,* May 1986, pp. 53-58. Similarly, Robert Sullivan, Director of Research in the governor's office, noted, "The New York metropolitan suburbs are the most important, but the suburbs in some of the upstate cities are very important also. They are of secondary importance only because of their size...." Interview on September 8, 1986.

[3]Kevin P. Phillips, *The Emerging Republican Majority* (New York: Arlington House, 1969) pg. 39.

[4]Everett Carll Ladd with Charles D. Hadley, *Transformations of the American Party System,* 2nd ed. (New York: W.W. Norton & Company, Inc., 1978) pg. 3.

[5]Warren E. Miller and Teresa E. Levitin, *Leadership and Change: The New Politics and the American Electorate* (Cambridge, MA: Winthrop Publishers, 1976) pg. 22.

[6]Frederick M. Wirt, Benjamin Walter, Francine F. Rabinovitz, Deborah R. Hensler, *On the City's Rim: Politics and Policy in Suburbia* (Lexington, MA: D.C. Heath and Co., 1972) pg. 51.

[7]*Ibid.,* pg. 52.

[8]Robert C. Wood, *Suburbia: Its People and Their Politics* (Boston, MA: Houghton Mifflin Co., 1958) pg. 148.

[9]*U.S. News and World Report*, March 12, 1984, pg. 59. Compiled by their economic unit from the 1980 Census.

[10]"The Suburban Voter: Which Way Does He Lean?" *Newsweek*, April 1, 1957, pg. 42.

[11]*Ibid.*

[12]Jerome M. Clubb, Erik W. Austin and Michael W. Traugott, "Demographic and Compositional Change," in Jerome M. Clubb, William H. Flanigan and Nancy H. Zingale, eds., *Analyzing Electoral History: A Guide to the Study of American Voter Behavior* (Beverly Hills: Sage Publications, 1981) pg. 116.

[13]Ladd, *op. cit.*, pg. XX.

[14]Phillips, *op. cit.*, pg. 176.

[15]Ladd, *op. cit.*, pg. 95.

[16]*Ibid.*, pg. 98.

[17]Richard M. Scammon and Ben J. Wattenberg, *The Real Majority* (New York: Coward, McCann, 1970).

[18]Morris Janowitz, *The Last Half-Century: Societal Change and Politics in America* (Chicago: University of Chicago Press, 1978) pg. 169.

[19]David S. Broder, "Introduction," in Seymour Martin Lipset, ed., *Party Coalitions in the 1980's* (San Francisco: Institute for Contemporary Studies, 1981) pg. 7.

[20]A. James Reichley, "As Go the Suburbs, So Goes U.S. Politics," *Fortune*, September 1970, pg. 108.

[21]*Ibid.*

[22]"Our Changing Suburbs," *The New York Times*, August 22, 1955, pg. 20.

[23]Regional Plan Association Report as discussed in "Post-War Job Rise Shows Lag in City," *The New York Times*, November 28, 1954, pg. 26.

[24]Edith Evans Asbury, "Our Changing City: Nassau-Suffolk Area of Long Island," *The New York Times*, August 19, 1955, pg. 21.

[25]*Ibid.*

[26]Peter O. Muller, *Contemporary Suburban America* (Englewood Cliffs, NJ: Prentice-Hall Inc., 1981) pg. 6.

[27]New York State Department of Labor, "Annual Planning Information for Manpower Planners: New York Suburban District," Fiscal Year 1983, pp. 19, 25.

[28]Andrew M. Hamer, "Perspectives on Urban Atlanta," *Atlanta Economic Review*, vol. 28, January/February 1978, pg. 6.

[29]William Severini Kowinski, "Suburbia: End of the Golden Age," *The New York Times Magazine*, March 16, 1980, pg. 19.

120

[30]New York State Department of Labor, "Commuting in the New York City Metropolitan Area 1970 and 1980," Bureau of Labor Market Information Report #9, 1984, pp. 8, 11.

[31]*Ibid.,* pg. 19.

[32]Muller, *op. cit.,* pg. 4.

[33]James Feron, Richard L. Madden and Robert Reinhold, analysis of *The New York Times* suburban poll, *The New York Times,* November 13, 1978, pp. B1, B4; November 14, 1978, pg. B3; November 15, 1978, pg. B4; November 16, 1978, pg. B4.

[34]*Ibid.*

[35]Louis H. Masotti, "The Suburban Seventies," *Annals of the American Academy of Political and Social Science,* 42 (1975), pg. vii.

[36]Muller, *op. cit.,* pg. 3.

[37]Feron, *et al., op. cit.*

Footnotes for Chapter Three

[1]Unless otherwise noted, references to MIPO data on the suburbs are drawn from an attitudinal survey of 1049 registered suburban voters conducted in September 1985.

[2]Angus Campbell, Philip E. Converse, Warren E. Miller, and Donald E. Stokes, *The American Voter* (New York: Wiley, 1960) pg. 143.

[3]Walter Dean Burnham, *Critical Elections and the Mainsprings of American Politics* (New York: W.W. Norton & Company, 1970) pp. 128, 130.

[4]Paul R. Abramson, *Political Attitudes in America: Formation and Change* (San Francisco: W.H. Freeman & Co., 1983) pg. 11.

[5]Warren E. Miller and Teresa E. Levitin, *Leadership and Change: The New Politics and the American Electorate* (Cambridge, MA: Winthrop Publishers, Inc., 1976) pg. 99.

[6]William Crotty, *American Parties in Decline,* 2nd ed. (Boston: Little, Brown & Company, 1984) pg. 37.

[7]Clarence Dean, "Disunity in GOP Reflects New Structure of Suburbs," *The New York Times,* June 1, 1964, pg. 1.

[8]Calculations include districts with boundaries which extend beyond the county lines of the New York suburbs.

[9]New York State Survey of 600 registered voters, Marist Institute for Public Opinion, Marist College, January 1985.

Footnotes for Chapter Four

[1]Frank Lynn, "Cuomo Beats Koch in Democratic Primary," *The New York Times,* September 24, 1982, pg. 1.

[2]Frank Lynn, "Cuomo Claims Victory in Tight Race," *The New York Times,* November 3, 1982, pg. 1.

[3]Andrew O'Rourke interviewed by Joseph Laura, "The Man Who Would Be Governor," *Empire State Report,* August 1986, pg. 44.

[4]Alan R. Gitelson, M. Margaret Conway and Frank B. Feigert, *American Political Parties: Stability and Change* (Boston: Houghton, Mifflin Co., 1984) pg. 34.

[5]John G. Stewart, "The Democratic Party in American Politics," in Jeff Fishel, ed., *Parties and Elections in an Anti-Party Age* (Bloomington, Indiana: Indiana University Press, 1978) pg. 72.

[6]William Crotty, ed., *The Party Symbol* (San Francisco: W.H. Freeman & Company, 1980) pg. 221.

[7]James L. Sundquist, *Dynamics of the Party System,* rev. ed. (Washington, DC: The Brookings Institution, 1983) pg. 350.

[8]Everett Carll Ladd, "The Shifting Party Coalitions—from the 1930's to the 1970's," in Seymour M. Lipset, ed., *Party Coalitions in the 1980s* (San Francisco: Institute for Contemporary Studies, 1981) pg. 137.

[9]Richard Jenson, "The Last Party System: Decay of Consensus, 1932-1980," in Paul Kleppner *et al., The Evolution of American Electoral Systems,* Contributions in American History #95 (Westport, CT: Greenwood Press, 1981) pg. 204.

[10]Gallup Poll results as compiled in the Baron Report, January 14, 1985, pg. 3.

[11]Mario Cuomo, *Inside Albany,* November 10, 1984.

[12]Mark Penn, *Inside Albany,* November 10, 1984.

[13]Interview with Timothy Russert, February 20, 1986.

[14]Interview with Gary Fryer, September 8, 1986.

[15]Alan Chartock, "How'd You Like To Be In These Guys' Shoes?" *Poughkeepsie Journal,* August 25, 1986, pg. 5A.

[16]Mario Cuomo, *Inside Albany,* September 22, 1985.

[17]Interview with Gerald Crotty, September 8, 1986.

[18]Interview with Governor Mario Cuomo, March 5, 1986.

[19]*Ibid.*

[20]Russert, *op. cit.*

[21]Mary McGrory, "Cuomo: Democrats' Last Left '88 Hope," *The Washington Post National Weekly,* November 11, 1984, pg. D1.

[22]Mario Cuomo, *Inside Albany,* November 10, 1984.

Footnotes for Chapter Five

[1]Richard C. Niemi and Herbert F. Weisberg, *Controversies in American Voting Behavior* (San Francisco: W.H. Freeman and Company, 1976) pg. 362.

[2]Kevin P. Phillips, *The Emerging Republican Majority* (New York: Arlington House, 1969) pg. 65.

[3]"The New Cycle in Politics: Break in Democratic Coalition," *The United States News,* November 15, 1946, pg. 13.

[4]"Fulbright Invites Truman to Resign," *The New York Times,* November 7, 1946.

[5]"Effects of New Deal Victory," *U.S. News and World Report,* July 23, 1948, pg. 19.

[6]William S. White, "Sweep in Congress," *The New York Times,* November 4, 1948, pg. 1.

[7]Louis Harris, *Is There a Republican Majority?* (New York: Harper & Brothers, 1954).

[8]James Reston, "President's Power Breaks Democrats' Grip on Cities," *The New York Times,* November 8, 1956, pg. 1.

[9]Angus Campbell, "Interpreting the Presidential Victory," in Milton Cummings, Jr., ed., *The National Election of 1964* (Washington, DC: The Brookings Institution, 1966) pg. 281.

[10]Phillips, *op. cit.,* pg. 23.

[11]Niemi and Weisberg, *op. cit.,* pg. 363.

[12]James L. Sundquist, "Whither the American Party System?" in Jeff Fishel, ed., *Parties and Elections in an Anti-Party Age* (Bloomington, Indiana: Indiana University Press, 1978) pg. 342.

[13]David S. Broder, "Introduction," in Seymour Martin Lipset, ed., *Party Coalitions in the 1980s* (San Francisco: Institute for Contemporary Studies, 1981) pg. 5.

[14]Richard M. Scammon and Ben J. Wattenberg, "Is it the End of an Era?" *Public Opinion,* October/November 1980, pg. 3.

[15]David S. Broder, "A Sharp Right Turn: Republicans and Democrats Alike See New Era in '80 Returns," *The Washington Post,* November 6, 1980, pg. A1.

[16]Dan Balz, "The GOP As Majority Party?" *The Washington Post National Weekly,* January 28, 1985, pg. 11.

[17]Benjamin Ginsberg and Martin Shefter, "A Critical Realignment? The New Politics, the Reconstituted Right, and the Election of 1984," in Michael Nelson, ed., *The Election of 1984* (Washington, DC: Congressional Quarterly Press, 1985) pg. 23.

[18]Phillips, *op. cit.*, pg. 39.

[19]Jerome M. Clubb, William H. Flanigan and Nancy H. Zingale, *Partisan Realignment*, Sage Library of Social Research, 108 (Beverly Hills: Sage Publications, 1980) pg. 21.

[20]James L. Sundquist, *Dynamics of the Party System*, rev. ed. (Washington, DC: The Brookings Institution, 1983) pg. 15.

[21]John R. Petrocik, *Party Coalitions* (Chicago: The University of Chicago Press, 1981) pg. 25.

[22]Paul Kleppner, et al., *The Evolution of American Electoral Systems*, Contributions in American History #95 (Westport, CT: Greenwood Press, 1981) pg. 5.

[23]"Closing the Gap," *Time*, April 22, 1957, pg. 29.

[24]Cited in Kevin P. Phillips, *Post-Conservative America* (New York: Random House, 1982) pg. 58.

[25]James L. Sundquist, "Whither the American Party System?—Revisited," *Political Science Quarterly*, 98:4 (Winter 1983/1984) pg. 584.

[26]Adam Clymer, "Poll Finds Nation is Becoming Increasingly Republican," *The New York Times*, May 3, 1981, pg. 1.

[27]Adam Clymer and Kathleen Frankovic, "The Realities of Realignment," *Public Opinion*, June/July 1981, pg. 42.

[28]"GOP Closes on Democrats," *The Washington Post National Weekly*, December 17, 1984, pg. 38.

[29]*Ibid.*

[30]William Crotty, *American Parties in Decline*, 2nd ed. (Boston: Little, Brown & Company, 1984) pg. 27.

[31]Sundquist, *Dynamics*, pg. 436.

[32]Sundquist, "Whither the American Party System?—Revisited," pg. 577.

[33]Thomas B. Edsall, "The GOP Push for Converts in Four States," *The Washington Post National Weekly*, May 27, 1985, pg. 11.

[34]R.W. Apple, "President Highly Popular in Poll; No Ideological Shift is Discerned," *The New York Times*, January 28, 1986, pg. A14.

[35]Steven V. Roberts, "Democrats Told Voters are Drifting Back to Party," *The New York Times*, February 20, 1986, pg. 20.

[36]Everett Carll Ladd, "Realignment? No. Dealignment? Yes." *Public Opinion*, October/November 1980, pg. 15.

[37]Phillips, *Post-Conservative America*, pg. 224.

[38]William Schneider quoted in "The Tapestry of Election '84," *Newsweek*, November 19, 1984, pg. 58.

[39]Everett Carll Ladd with Charles D. Hadley, *Transformations of the American Party System,* 2nd ed. (New York: W.W. Norton & Company, Inc., 1978) pg. 378.

[40]"End of the Democratic Era?" *Newsweek,* August 18, 1980, pg. 21.

[41]David S. Broder, "Victory Shows Broad Appeal of President," *The Washington Post,* November 7, 1984, pg. 1.

[42]Walter Dean Burnham, "The Eclipse of the Democratic Party," *Society,* July/August 1984, pg. 5.

[43]*Ibid.*

[44]Richard Harwood, "Middle Class Gave Victory," *The Washington Post,* November 7, 1984, pg. A29.

[45]Adam Clymer, "Poll Finds Reagan Failed to Obtain a Policy Mandate," *The New York Times,* November 12, 1984, pp. 1, 30, cited in Walter Dean Burnham, "The Future of American Politics," in Ellis Sandoz and Cecil V. Crabb, Jr., eds., *Election '84: Landslide Without a Mandate?* (New York: New American Library, 1985).

[46]William Schneider, "Half a Realignment," *The New Republic,* December 3, 1984, pg. 19.

[47]George Will, "Realignment Is a Fact," *The Washington Post,* November 8, 1985, pg. A27.

[48]"Mondale-Ferraro Bandwagon Turns Right," *U.S. News and World Report,* August 13, 1984, pg. 7.

[49]Walter Mondale quoted in "The Challenger's Outlook," *Newsweek,* November 5, 1984, pg. 29.

[50]Bernard Weinraub, "Mondale Shifting Focus From Deficit," *The New York Times,* October 18, 1984, pg. D27.

[51]Thomas Ferguson and Joel Rogers, "Why Mondale Turned Right," *The Nation,* October 6, 1984, pg. 313.

[52]Schneider, "Half a Realignment," pg. 21.

[53]Morris P. Fiorina, *Retrospective Voting in American National Elections* (New Haven: Yale University Press, 1981).

[54]Seymour Martin Lipset, *Party Coalitions in the 1980s,* pg. XIV.

[55]Curtis B. Gans, "Conservatism By Default," *The Nation,* October 14, 1978, pg. 373.

[56]Adam Clymer, "Public Prefers a Balanced Budget to Large Cut in Taxes, Poll Shows," *The New York Times,* February 3, 1981, pg. A1.

[57]David E. Price, *Bringing Back the Parties* (Washington, DC: Congressional Quarterly Press, 1984) pg. 8.

[58]Barry Sussman, "Behind Reagan's Popularity: A Little Help From His Foes," *The Washington Post National Weekly,* February 4, 1985, pg. 37.

[59]Adam Clymer, "Poll Finds Reagan Failed to Obtain a Policy Mandate," pp. 1, 30.

[60]*The Gallup Report,* June 1985, pp. 4, 5.

[61]Barry Sussman, "The Public Perceives a Stalemate in Reagan's War on Waste," *The Washington Post National Weekly,* September 2, 1985, pg. 37.

[62]R.W. Apple, *op. cit.,* pg. 1.

[63]*Ibid.*

[64]Price, *op. cit.,* pg. 9.

[65]William H. Flanigan and Nancy H. Zingale, *Political Behavior of the American Electorate,* 5th ed. (Boston: Allyn and Bacon, Inc., 1983).

[66]Heritage Foundation poll conducted May 28-July 8, 1985.

[67]R.W. Apple, *op. cit.,* pg. A14.

[68]William Crotty, *op. cit.,* pp. 68-69.

[69]Sundquist, *Dynamics,* pg. 440.

[70]Clubb *et al., op. cit.,* pg. 37.

[71]Warren Moscow, "Democrats Shy At Leftists But Won't Go Conservative," *The New York Times,* November 7, 1946, pg. 1.

[72]Key, V.O., *The Responsible Electorate* (Cambridge, MA: Harvard University Press, 1966) pg. 2.

[73]Interview with Carl Leubsdorf, Washington, D.C. bureau chief, *The Dallas Morning News,* April 21, 1986.

[74]Mario Cuomo interviewed by Judy Watson, "The View From Albany," *Empire State Report,* December 1985, pg. 12.

[75]Interview with Carl Leubsdorf.

[76]Mario Cuomo, *Inside Albany,* January 4, 1986.

[77]Maurice Carroll, "Cuomo Wants to Go Beyond Workfare to the Work Ethic," *The New York Times,* January 1986, Sec. IV, and "Cuomo, a Liberal, Tries a Conservative Theme," *The New York Times,* January 18, 1986, pg. 30.